'Its Own Way of Things'

Published by: Lagan Press/Linen Hall Library

ISBN: 1-904652-19-0

Editor: Odling-Smee, Hugh

Title: Its Own Way of Things
A Celebration of the Ulster Literary Theatre
2004

Front Cover: Reproduction from first edition of *Ulad* (1904)

Cover Design: December Publications

Printed by: Easyprint, Belfast

Lagan Press
1A Bryson Street, Belfast BT5 4ES

Linen Hall Library
17 Donegall Square North, Belfast BT1 5GB

The Linen Hall Library

Theatre & Performing Arts Archive

and Lagan Press present

'Its Own Way of Things'

a celebration of the Ulster Literary Theatre

edited by Hugh Odling-Smee

The Enthusiast

by Lewis Purcell

introduced by Mark Phelan

Thompson in Tir-na-nOg

by Gerald MacNamara

introduced by John McCann

linen hall library established 1788

LAGAN PRESS

arts council of Northern Ireland LOTTERY FUNDED

Queen's University Belfast

Lyric Theatre

An unkown ULT production featuring Harry Morrow (right seated) and Fred Morrow (right standing).

Preface

The Linen Hall Library Theatre & Performing Arts Archive was created in 1996 in order to collect and promote the history of our cultural life in Northern Ireland. The Archive dedicates itself to ensuring that our rich cultural heritage is not lost, but rather serves to encourage and inspire those who work in and study the performing arts both today and tomorrow. In this spirit, we present to you *Its Own Way of Things.*

This publication is a celebration of the 100th anniversary of the first performances of the Ulster Literary Theatre. These performances took place in the Ulster Minor Hall (later the Group Theatre) on 7th December 1904. Two plays were performed that day, *The Reformers* written by David Parkhill under the pen name of Lewis Purcell and *Brian of Banba* by Bulmer Hobson. Both men had attempted to launch an Ulster branch of the Irish Literary Theatre of Lady Gregory and W.B. Yeats. In this endeavour they were rebuffed and so, in 1904, they renamed their organisation the Ulster Literary Theatre, Ulster's first independent theatre company.

The ULT did not last forever with the financial pressure to turn a profit eventually spelling its end in 1940. Its bloodline however, can be seen to be flourishing today. The history of Northern Irish theatre is full of companies seeing a need and filling a void. From the Belfast Repertory Theatre Company to the Ulster Group, the Lyric Players to Charabanc, from Tinderbox to the young Turks of today, the impulse to reflect and shape the society we see around us through the theatre remains the same as it was in 1904. The ULT left us with the knowledge that we could express our particular genius on the stage and be accepted both by our own people and those in foreign fields.

This document contains reprints of two of the ULT's most influential and successful plays, *Thompson in Tir-na-nOg* by Gerald MacNamara and *The Enthusiast* by Lewis Purcell. Both plays are introduced by two young theatre practitioners: John McCann, the Outreach Director of Tinderbox Theatre Company and Mark Phelan, Lecturer in Drama at the Queen's University. The archive is extremely grateful for their time and efforts. Also gratefully included is Ophelia Byrne's rigorously researched list of the premieres of the ULT. We have also reprinted, by way of adding context, the manifesto of Ulad, the short-lived organ of the ULT.

To be sincerely thanked are Patrick Ramsey of Lagan Press and Jake Campbell of December Publications. To Mrs Brigid Ferguson, we extend our thanks for permission to re-print *Thompson in Tir-na-nOg*, and her continued support of the work of the archive. To Irish Playography many thanks are due for allowing us to reprint some of Ophelia Byrne's exhaustive research. Finally thanks especially to Jane Moore and all the staff of the Linen Hall Library.

We hope you enjoy this document, which in some small way we hope rekindles the memory of those interesting Edwardian men and women whose artistic impulse still burns brightly on stages across this country.

Hugh Odling-Smee
Curator, Theatre & Performing Arts Archive
Linen Hall Library, Belfast

Ulad

Ulad was the literary magazine of the Ulster Literary Theatre and was published four times from November 1904 to September 1905. Its editors were J.W. Reynolds and David Parkhill, who recruited writers such as Forrest Reid, William Donn, Alice L Milligan, Francis Joseph Bigger and almost all the major artistic figures of the early twentieth century in Ulster. The magazine featured intense articles on national revival beside light pieces on house-painting.*

This extract, from the first issue, is what stood as a manifesto for the movement. Self-consciously radical, the statements that follow caused much controversy at their time of publication. It is re-published here in order to give a sense of the confidence of the movement and the energy from which the Ulster Literary Theatre sprang.

Ulad means Ulster. It is often necessary to state as much; we intend to insist. Draw an imaginary line across Ireland from that great bight, Donegal Bay, in the west, to Carlingford Lough, on the East, and draw it not too rigidly; north of that you have Ulster. This Ulster has its own way of things, which may be taken as the great contrast to the Munster way of things, still keeping on Irish lands.

Cities like Londonderry and Belfast have drawn all its best energies towards them. And though of late years the city has been more a stumbling-block to the right intellectual and artistic progress of the country. Yet in spite of influences and disabilities operating against it, a certain characteristic temperamental and mental trend has been lent to the town by the country, and a certain local intellectual activity has persisted there. We wish to locate this, and to afford it an outlet in literary expression.

Exactly what that local temperament and artistic aptitude are *Ulad* wants to discuss. *Ulad* would also influence them, direct and inform them. And as the Theatre is the most essential of art activities, and the surest test of a people's emotional and intellectual vitality, *Ulad* starts out as an organ of the Theatre, the Ulster Literary Theatre, but proposes to be as irrelevant to that movement and its topics as is deemed necessary.

While any other provocation would serve, we may as well use that which the Greeks, the Elizabethans, the contemporaries of Moliere, and the Norway of Ibsen have utilised to such great purpose. So we intend to strike our keynote through the theatre where our own plays will be produced, and to let that discover our pathway for us and voice those aims and hopes and hatreds and loves best expressed that way. *Ulad* follows, directs, comments, suggests, or discourages, just as our better conscience dictates.

We recognise at the outset that our art of the drama will be different from that other Irish art of drama which speaks from the stage of the Irish National Theatre in Dublin, where two men, W.B. Yeats and Douglas Hyde, have set a model in Anglo-Irish and Gaelic plays with a success that is surprising and exhilarating. Dreamer, mystic, symbolist, Gaelic poet and propagandist have all spoken on the Dublin stage, and a fairly defined local school has been inaugurated. We in Belfast and Ulster also wish to set up a school; but there will be a difference.

At present we can only say our talent is more satiric than poetic. That will probably remain the broad difference between the Ulster and the Leinster schools. But when our genius arrives, as he must sooner or later, there is no accounting for what extraordinary tendency he may display. Our business is however, to plod along gathering matter for his use, practising methods, perfecting technique, and training actors.

We hope to publish a short play with each number. These plays will all be by Ulster writers living in Ulster or elsewhere. A page or more will be devoted to Gaelic, and the rest of the magazine to essays, short poems, and illustrations. It is hoped in the critical portion to cover the whole of Ulster local activates; thought, art, art-industry, music, architecture, and literature, seen through the eyes, the enthusiasms, the impressions of the younger men principally, of whom we have most to hope and most to fear.

We have most to fear for the young men in that, if they do not find an outlet in Ulster, they will either go away, or gravitate upon the sloblands of American or English magazine work, which is purely commercial and has no pretension to literature whatever. It expresses nothing, means nothing; it aims at being sixpence worth. We do not aim at being sixpence worth; we aim at being priceless, for honesty and good purpose are priceless. If we do not attain to all this, we shall at least attain to something unique in Ulster, smacking of the soil, the winds on the uplands, the north coast, the sun and the rain, and the long winter evenings.

Ulad will be non-sectarian and non-political; each article will be signed by the writer as an expression of his own individual views; other views may be put forward in an other number. In any case, our pages will be kept free from the party-cries of mob and clique and marketplace. Honesty in all matters of taste and opinion will, we hope, characterise our matter. Our contributors are mostly young men, of all sects and all grades of political opinion.

The journal will be run on broad propagandist lines. Propagandism on broad lines, we think, is desirable at this juncture. There is a strong undercurrent of culture in the North, and this we will endeavour to tap, and, if possible, turn into native channels. As a good Ulsterman, and a friend of this venture, has truly said: 'We effect a great deal – the voice of the press is far reaching. We may roll the stone that has been only pushed at by others. Then will the heroes of the North ride forth again; at present they only sleep within the cavern of dark prejudice and ignorance and distrust.'

If we succeed in accomplishing this much, if we roll the stone, if it is in our power to awaken the heroes to activity and the people to sympathy and life, surely our existence will be justified.

Sketches of *The Enthusiast* characters by Norman Morrow (reproduced courtesy of Mrs Brigid Ferguson).

RAB.

"I was crackin' to a wheen o' girls."

WILLIAM JOHN M'KINSTRY.

"Cooperation d'ye say?"

The Enthusiast(s)

by **Mark Phelan**
Lecturer in Drama, Queens University, Belfast

'In those days, Belfast had little appetite for plays of ideas or drama that dealt with 'subjects'. I think the preference was for the matinee idol and musical comedy..."[1]

The eponymous idealism of Lewis Purcell's (David Parkhill) 1905 play appositely describes the cast of enthusiasts that formed the Ulster Literary Theatre. Parkhill, co-founded the ULT along with the quixotic Quaker republican Bulmer Hobson, to provide a, 'commentary on the political and social conditions of the North of Ireland.'[2] Although, at first, this new 'artistic and liberalising movement'[3] functioned merely as a corollary of the Irish Literary Theatre,[4] it later evolved a critique of its southern counterpart and developed a prescient regio-national narrative of Northern identity, that anticipated many of the later discourses of different critical and cultural movements.

Parkhill's first play, *The Reformers*, a 'smart, spicy, comedy *exposé*'[5] of municipal jobbery, launched the ULT 1904 when it was produced with Bulmer Hobson's *Brian of Banba*. His second play, *The Enthusiast*, produced in May 1905 with Joseph Campbell's *The Little Cowherd of Slainge*, marked a milestone in the artistic development of the theatre, 'both in the expression of ideas and the handling of technique.'[6] *The Enthusiast* deals with the efforts

1 Joseph Connolly, *The Memoirs of Senator Joseph Connolly (1885-1961): A Founder of Modern Ireland*, ed. J.A. McGaughan (Dublin: Irish Academic Press, 1996), 59.

2 Bulmer Hobson, *Ireland: Yesterday and Tomorrow* (Tralee: Anvil Books, 1968), 4.

3 Arthur Griffith, 'All Ireland', *The United Irishman*, 31 December 1904.

4 The Irish Literary Theatre (1899-1902), later known as the Irish National Dramatic Society (1902-4), the Irish National Theatre Society (1904-6) and the National Theatre Society Limited (1906-).

5 *Nomad's Weekly and Belfast Critic*, 24 December 1904.

6 *Northern Whig*, 5 May 1905.

of Jamie McKinstry, an idealistic farmer's son who returns home from the city, to unite local Catholic and Protestant farmers under the ideological auspices of the co-operative agricultural movement. Jamie's attempt to proselytise Ultonian farmers to his utopian vision of agricultural co-operation is crushed as a local community meeting called to discuss the project disintegrates into internecine sectarian conflict. The play concludes with the disillusioned hero 'sitting dejectedly alone, the last remnant of spirit crushed out of him by the sound of drums in the distant night.'[7]

Whilst *The Reformers* was acclaimed as 'an Ibsenic comedy without any of the great dramatist's dolefulness,'[8] some reviewers singled out this latter quality in *The Enthusiast* for criticism. The Ibsenite pessimism of its *denouement*, whereby the 'enthusiast' is rejected as the 'enemy of the people' and fatalistically acquiesces to the defeat of his 'superior' idealism by sectarian atavism, was condemned by poet Patrick Colum as 'immoral'. Local critics, however, were more fulsome in their praise: the novelist Forrest Read wrote an open letter to the *Northern Whig*, extolling the play as, 'infinitely superior to any modern play... seen in Belfast', 'a little work of art worth a hundred of the productions of Pineros and Joneses we are so frequently asked to applaud today,'[9] and exhorted local audiences of Lineopolis to lend their support to the ULT. Other critics celebrated Parkhill's efforts to tackle an urgent political issue and praised his:

> selection of a theme, and without affectation or pretence at preaching he manages in the space of two short scenes, to restate with boldness and originality, the central problem which Ireland has to solve in the near future if she is to preserve her national identity and attain to that high destiny which her sons, whatever views they may hold, unite in believing the future holds in store.'[10]

7 Joseph Power, 'The Ulster Literary Theatre', *Ulad*, I/4 (Sept. 1905), 6.

8 *Nomad's Weekly and Belfast Critic*, 17 December 1904.

9 *Northern Whig*, 5 May 1905.

10 *Northern Whig*, 5 May 1905.

Indeed, the play explicitly advocates the progressive politics 'sweeping the country' of Sir Horace Plunkett's Irish Agricultural Organisation Society (IAOS), which sought to steer a third way between the Scylla and Charybdis of nationalist and unionist politics. Historian Roy Foster's description of the IAOS as a 'conciliationist'[11] movement, is certainly reflected in the heterogeneous composition of its central committee, convened by Plunkett and comprising Liberal and Tory Peers, Parnellitte factions, prominent Orangemen, a Jesuit educationist, northern industrialists and the nationalist and unionist mayors of Belfast and Dublin! This miraculous collective Plunkett modestly called a 'strange council' but which might 'fairly claim to be representative in every material respect'.[12] In spite of bitter political differences the IAOS managed to secure a new Department of Agriculture and Technical Instruction for Ireland in 1899, in effect, creating a *de facto* home rule for Irish agriculture[13] and this new department sought to modernise Irish agriculture by improving farming techniques, introducing new technologies and forming co-operative organisations of small farmers. Plunkett documents in his efforts to transform Irish agriculture into an efficient and technically proficient enterprise in his visionary treatise, *Ireland in the New Century* (1904): a work redolent of Jamie McKinstry's rhetoric:

> We are on the eve of the creation of a peasant proprietary, involving the rehabilitation of rural life, and one essential condition of the successful inauguration of the new agrarian order is the elimination of anything approaching to sectarian bitterness in communities...[14]

However, Jamie's fickle idealism is as much the object of Parkhill's satire as the sectarianism of the local community, for Jamie's commitment to his cause compares unfavourably with Plunkett's. As another co-operative 'Enthusiast' and Ulsterman, George Russell (AE) records: 'He [Plunkett] had fifty

11 Roy Foster, *Modern Ireland 1600-1972* (London: Penguin, 1989), 434.

12 Horace Plunkett, *Ireland in the New Century* (London: John Murray, 1904), 218.

13 P.J. Mathews, *Revival: The Abbey Theatre, Sinn Fein, The Gaelic League and the Co-operative Movement* (Cork: Cork University Press, 2003), 9. This process was also assisted by new legislation and administrative reforms: The Congested Districts Board (1890), Local Government Act (1898) Wyndham's Land Act (1903), all helped pave the way for the 'relatively smooth transition from British rule to the political independence of the Irish Free State'. Lionel Pilkington, *Theatre and State in Twentieth Century Ireland: Cultivating the People* (London: Routledge, 2001), 3.

14 Plunkett, *Ireland in the New Century*, 100.

unsuccessful meetings before he could get the first farmer's creamery started'. Plunkett had also demonstrated little of the naivety of Jamie and tackled sectarianism head on, even appealing to it to secure cross-community agreement!

> He said a few weeks ago in Belfast at a public meeting where he tried to melt the obdurate sectarianism with a little humour. 'We all know that those who differ from us on matters of religion will be adequately punished in the hereafter. So why harbour bad feeling now?'[15]

However, it is the aesthetics rather than the politics of *The Enthusiast* that are important. Its dialogue marked the ULT's rejection of the pseudo-Synge-song grandiloquence favoured by their southern counterparts in favour of what Tom Paulin evocatively calls the 'scutching vernacular' of Ulster speech. This contrast is starkly evident in the May 1905 ULT productions: *The Enthusiast's* naturalistic dialogue is dramatically different from the florid speechifying of Campbell's play. Compare the *Cowherd's* stilted diction: 'I would speak with thee, woman. How is thy care? Ah woman, I like not thy looks. Thou turnest the white of thine eye to me. Thou art wan as a witch-wife strange thing in this tanning sun and whole-some southerly air,'[16] with the clattery speech of *The Enthusiast*: 'I knowed fine there wuz somethin' up wi' him. Naebody iver heered the likes o' the talk he wuz goin' on wi' afore you came in. Jamie McKinstry, ye shud be weel ashamed o' yourself.'[17]

When *The Enthusiast* received a second production at the Toome Feis in Co, Antrim in 1905, along with *Brian of Banba*, the farmers and pollen-fishers of the audience were 'bored' by *Brian*; their incomprehension of Hobson's inflated language mirrored that felt by William John McKinstry for his enthusiast son's educated talk: 'Why did ye no' tell it to me in plain language? How wuz *I* to make sense o' your high-falutin' talk?'[18]

15 *Letters from AE*, ed. Alan Denson, (London: Abelard-Scuman, 1961) 37.

16 Joseph Campbell, *The Little Cowherd of Slainge, Ulad* I/I, (Nov. 1904), 24.

17 David Parkhill, *The Enthusiast, Ulad* I/3, (May 1905), 30.

18 *The Enthusiast*, 34.

Indeed, these lines struck a chord with the ULT who recognized that their audience's disinterest in *Brian* was matched by their delight in the 'homely touches of type, local idiom and situation' of *The Enthusiast*. The play's Chaucer-cum-Burns composite speech of English, Irish and Ulster-Scots had a remarkable affect on local audiences, for this was the first time that Ulster peasantry had ever been represented onstage:

> I was interested enough in *Brian of Banba*... But what really did impress me was *The Enthusiast*, because for the first time I saw the kind of people that I knew and lived among in Co. Antrim and Co. Derry were there alive and talking as they talked at home.[19]

The success of *The Enthusiast* encouraged the ULT to aesthetically develop the regionalist ideology articulated in its literary journal *Ulad*. The vast majority of their work, thus features an Ulster *mise-en-scène* whilst their 'manipulation of a singularly barbarous dialect',[20] as one English critic opined, became a key dramaturgical feature of their work. Parkhill's play was of seminal importance to this development of a regionalist realism, which radiated an altogether different PQ from that of the Abbey's 'Peasant Quality': a Protestant Quality, as against the background of increasing emphases on Gaelic, Catholic and rural aspects of 'Irishness', the *dramatis personae* of the ULT's plays were predominantly Protestant!

In an interview, many years later, when questioned on the 'confused history' of the ULT, Rutherford Mayne was remarkably candid in his response:

> Don't forget that even to the end – ten or twelve years ago – we were always under a bit of a cloud... After all, when you've a flaming nationalist like Bulmer Hobson or Joe Campbell, or Francis Joseph Biggar (*sic*) as a member of your society, it takes lot of explaining

19 *Enter Robbie John*, written and complied by David Kennedy, BBC Northern Ireland Region, 25 November, 1954, cited in Sam Hanna Bell, *The Theatre in Ulster*, (Dublin: Gill & Macmillan, 1972), 25.

20 Cited in Bell, *ibid*., 38.

> away. There wasn't much of Caesar's wife about us – even at the start. And that suspicion – although it wasn't always apparent – meant a good deal more than most of us cared to admit. But the suspicion was there – all the time.'[21]

Thus, *The Enthusiast* not only embodies early political philosophy and the cultural practice of the ULT, but provides a poignant epitaph for the demise of the theatre, as the 'miserable suspicion' indicted by the Enthusiast appears to have invidiously affected the ULT itself, in much the same way that it endures today.

21 'Meet Rutherford Mayne', *The Bell*, Ulster Issue' (July 1941) 246.

The Enthusiast

David Parkhill wrote under the name of Lewis Purcell. A major figure in the Ulster Revival, Parkhill co-edited *Ulad*, the magazine of the movement, and was the significant writer of the early years of the ULT. *The Reformers* (1904), *The Enthusiast* (1906) and *The Pagan* (1906) were instrumental in the creation of the 'Ulster Play'. He appeared to leave the movement around 1907, returning to contribute a single play *Cobbers Go Halves* in 1931. Little is known of his life. However, in his autobiography, Forrest Reid asserts that during the gap in contributions Parkhill spent time in the South Seas.

The Enthusiast (1906)

A comedy in two scenes

by Lewis Purcell

PEOPLE OF THE PLAY

William John McKinstry, a farmer.
James, his son, home from Belfast on vacation.
Sam, brother of James.
Aunt Margaret, housekeeper to her brother.
Minnie, engaged to James.
Rab, a servant man.

SCENE

A farm kitchen in southern portion of County Antrim. The left of stage is occupied by a large fire place having 'crane'. On one side of this is a door, leading to 'upper room'. On right side of stage a dressed, and beside it a door to bedroom. On back right, a door giving on to farmyard. On back centre, a deeply recessed window, and beneath it a table and chairs. An armchair in chimney corner, and over it a hanging lamp.

PERIOD

The Present Day.

First produced in the Clarence Place Hall, Belfast, 4th May, 1905 by members of the Ulster Literary Theatre.

Scene One

Dusk. Aunt Margaret is discovered tidying the hearth. She stops and looks in the direction of room left.

AUNT: He's a bigger swell every time he comes hame. Last year it wuz a white indiarubber tap coat. This time it's yella boots. But maybe he'll be wantin' a drap mair tay.

As she takes the teapot from the hob, James comes 'down' into the kitchen, wiping the crumbs from his waistcoat.

AUNT: Sure ye're no done? Ye tuk nothing at all!

JAMES: *standing with his back to the fire* Did I not? Then where did all that good thick fadge of yours go to? And the two fresh eggs? An the half print of butter? *Sits down in arm chair besides the fire, and folds his hands across his stomach* No, Aunt Margaret, there are no eggs like those in Belfast – nor tea like that.

AUNT: It's the came that does it.

JAMES: Nor there's no bread like yours anywhere – town or country.

AUNT: *pleased* Och, that's because you were hungry afther drivin' f'ae the station. But ye're no axin afther Minnie.

JAMES: Ah, I was just going to.

AUNT: She came ower in the fore part o' the day to see what time ye would be home. She'll be here ony minute, I'm thinkin'. Coming closer to him. Jamey, ye're no lukin' as strong as ordinary. Huh, ye've been powerin' ower your books again I expect. Ye shud hae mair sense. By the looks o' ye, it'll dae ye nae harm tae be gallivantin' aroun' the countryside for a while.

JAMES: No, there will be no gallivantin' this time, Aunt. I have lived long enough the life of a drone. I have been reading, as you say, but I have been thinking as well. I see how I can be of some use to humanity – on a very small scale of course; but it will always be something. I never understood before what was meant by the call of duty.

AUNT: *standing looking at him, puzzled* The call o' what? Of a' the talk!

JAMES: *smiling* You will understand all about it soon, Aunt Margaret, and perhaps you will have reason to be proud of me. I will spend my holiday this time labouring for an ideal – but it will be a labour of love.

During the latter part of this speech Minnie pushes the door open quietly and looks in. Then she enters and goes quickly over to James who rises to greet her.

MINNIE: *coyly* What's this talk of love, and me not here? Or maybe it was about me you were thinking?

JAMES: *taking her hands in his, and looking at her lovingly* God! You grow lovelier every day.

Aunt Margaret shakes her finger at them and then goes out. James takes Minnie in his arms and kisses her. She breaks away, and they sit together by the fire.

MINNIE: You didn't answer my question, sir.

JAMES: *puzzled* Eh?

MINNIE: You were talking about love when I came in, and *With mock displeasure* I'm sure it wasn't me you were speaking about.

JAMES: *laughing* No dear girl, it wasn't. It was about - a - but it's a long story. I'll tell you all about it tomorrow when we are alone.

MINNIE: *piqued* Oh!

James leans over and turns her face towards him. He looks at her a moment.

JAMES: Silly!

MINNIE: *with sudden gaiety* Oh James, I was nearly forgetting to tell you. The Milligans are giving a pic-nic party on the 24th, and I've got a new dress for it – Oh, if you saw me in that dress, dear, you would fall in love with me all over again. *Love business* Of course I have accepted for both of us.

JAMES: *doubtfully* Minnie, I don't see how I can go – my time will all be taken up –

MINNIE: *calmly* Nonsense; certainly you will go. You always say you won't go, but you always go to please me, dear, to please me. I know you don't care about company, but I do. And then the races are next week. And the bazaar is to be held in our meadow in tents. Oh, you'll be here for everything, and we'll have a grand time.

JAMES: *gently* Minnie, I tell you it's impossible, I can't go to any of those places. My mind is full of good work –

MINNIE: *interrupting* Do you really mean it? And my good dress is – lost! Oh, you don't – love me – any more. *Begins to weep. Then, recovering suddenly* Oh, very well, if you won't go with me there are dozens who would be glad of the chance.

JAMES: Don't be absurd, little girl; when you understand, you will not accuse me of that. I know that you will be the first to fall in with my plans and help me carry them out.

MINNIE: *angrily* Ah, I see how it is. There is someone else; some Belfast girl.

James makes a gesture of denial. During the forgoing speech Aunt enters, carrying a large iron pot. She sets it down in the middle of the floor and looks at James in astonishment.

AUNT: *bitterly* Ho, ho, that's it, is it? An' me aye blamin' it on the books. I knowed fine there was somethin' up wi him. *To Minnie* Naebody iver heard the likes o' the talk he wuz goin' on with afore you came in. *To James* Jamie McKinstry, ye shud be weel ahamed of yoursel', so you shud, you and your Belfast girls! I suppose they can play the pianna, an' smirk an' smile in drawin' room, an' talk book knowledge t'ye. I niver prophysied onythin very good o' ye' Jamie McKinstry, but I niver thought ye were goin to turn out a double-faced yin. Where ye get it, the Lord knows! It's no f'ae your father, a hard workin' sensible man, nor f'ae your poor mother that in her grave. That is what comes o' your readin'! *Emphatically* Jamie McKinstry, if I had a thousan' childer, the none o' them I wud wir let wihtin fifty mile o' any book.

JAMES: *holding up his hand in protest* But, Aunt Margaret, I assure you –

AUNT: *without heeding him* You an' your town girls! Show me yin o' them can make a steak pie or an' apple dumplin' along o' Minnie, a bake a griddle o' breed like her, or rich cakes or crumpets? Is there yin o' them fit herself out f'se heed to fut wi her ain hands, wi' a tailor-made? No yin o' them. *With disgust* Town girls! *Takes up pot again.*

JAMES: *despairingly, rising* Aunt Margaret, for heaven's sake will you let me explain –

AUNT: *going to the fire with pot* I'll no listen t'ye. I'll no listen t'ye.

MINNIE: *rising* I'm going home. *Moves towards the door.*

JAMES: *anxiously* I will go with you and tell you of my plans, and you will understand.

MIINIE: No, I will go alone.

JAMES: *determinedly* I am going to see you home.

MINNIE: *going out* I don't want your company.

James goes out after her. Aunt looks after them a moment, then sits down before the fire, thinking.

AUNT: *nodding her head* A Belfast girl, no less! Weel, weel, I niver thought he wud turn out like that. But the's somethin' else on his mind. Does he take a drap, I wonder. I niver seen ony signs o't on him. No, no, its them books has turned his heed. *Sighs* In my young day the' wuz none o' that. The boys stopped at hame, like his brother Sam there, and worked on the farm like honest men, in place of gallivantin about the town. *Rising* Ther's the rattle of wheels. They're early hame, it must ha' been a good market. *She goes out the door and looks out. Father and Sam enter carrying whips etc.*

AUNT: You're early back, William John.

FATHER: Aye it wuz a brave market for uplan'. I sowl baith loads inside twenty minutes at three and thruppence.

SAM: Did Jamie come?

AUNT: He did. He went to convey Minnie hame.

FATHER: *slyly* Oh aye. How's he in health?

AUNT: Bravely. But the's somethin' quare about him. He wuz talkin' the greatest clap-trap iver ye heard about – oh, I don' know whutit wuz about. Ye'll hear him at it yourself when he comes in. *She goes on with her work a moment, then stops.* An' he has broke wi' Minnie.

Father looks at her, and nods his head in surprise.

SAM: I don' know what Jamie iver seen in her onyway.

AUNT: *vehemently* She's a heap ower good for him, or you eather, Sam McKinstry.

FATHER: *holding up his hand* There, there, there. Whut wuz the trouble?

AUNT: Oh some town girl, I think.

FATHER: Aye, a town girl no less! They're a takin' wheen o' huzzies the Belfast yin's onyway. *Laughs to himself* I mind myself – in my young days – when I used to go to Belfast – *Thinks.*

SAM: *encouragingly* Aye?

FATHER: Ach – it's nothin'. But all the same, Minnie wud make him a good wife.

AUNT: A heap ower good for him.

James comes in, looking worried. His expression changes when he sees his father and brother. They rise to greet him.

SAM: Ha, Jamie.

FATHER: *looking at him curiously* Weel, my boy, ye ha' got hame for another wee while.

JAMES: Yes.

He sits down besides them and looks abstractedly into fire.

FATHER: Weel what's the news about Belfast?

JAMES: News? Ach, nothing worth talking about.

FATHER: Nobody dead or married or nothing?

JAMES: No.

SAM: Go on, man, and give us a bit of your crack. Cheer up, there's better girls nor her knocking about.

FATHER: What sort is she, this town girl?

JAMES: Town girl? I don't know what you're talking about.

SAM: Anyway, ther's no girl worth getting downhearted about.

JAMES: I'm not downhearted.

FATHER: Jimmie, there's something on your mind, you mostly have a lot to talk about when you come home.

JAMES: *rousing himself* And I have a lot to talk about this time also. Listen, I feel that I have a mission in life.

FATHER: A mission?

SAM: Sure, Jimmie, you're not turned religious, are you?

JAMES: Not at all, not at all. My head's full of a great idea.

FATHER: Full o'what?

JAMES: A great idea. I want to explain it to you. I have been reading and thinking a lot lately about the old village communities and wondering what would have been the logical outcome of that system in the present day. It was simply a sort of co-operation. And I believe that the same principle could be applied with great advantage. To everybody.

FATHER: Co-operation you say?

SAM: What's it about, Jamie?

JAMES: You know how bad farming is?

FATHER: Sowl, an' I do that!

JAMES: As it is at present everyone is working blindly for himself. Everyone has more work to do than he can accomplish if he wishes to get the best results from his land. Suppose now that a dozen farmers agreed to combine their farms and work them on a large scale, as they do, for instance, in America. You would find that, with properly organised labour, it could be made to pay with one half the sum of the work that is expended on the separate dozen farms. Do you follow me?

During the foregoing speech Rab comes in and stands listening curiously until the end. Then he sits down on chair beside table.

FATHER: Weel – I – it's a quare notion. *Thinks a moment. Then, suddenly to Rab* Did ye gie the horses their mash, Rab?

RAB: Aye and a drink and fothered them.

JAMES: *eagerly* That's the principle. Of course, it would take time. What I suggest is that, for the present, we try to form some sort of co-operative committee –

RAB: *interrupting* The's somthin' up wi' yin o' thew calves – the moyley's yin. She wudn't lip her drink the day nor yesterday. Dar' I try her with the patent feedin'?

SAM: Na, that patent stuff's weel enough for growing' heifers. I wouldn't want to try it on a three months calf.

JAMES: *who has been attempting to speak through all this impatiently* Listen, will you! What I was saying about the committee was –

FATHER: We're listenin' man. Go on.

JAMES: Well, the business of the committee would be to keep itself informed of all up-to-date farming methods. To disseminate a knowledge of this, and to assist in the formation co-operative societies throughout the district. To advise upon their mutual use, and to facilitate the export of your surplus produce, such as eggs, potatoes, fruit, pressed hay –

RAB: *to Sam* Did you bring the *Budget* wi' ye f'ae the town.

SAM: *taking it from his pocket* Aye, here it is. Watch an' no tear it. An' here's your *Christian Herald*, Aunt Margaret.

FATHER: *to James* Weel, is that the whole o't.

JAMES: *testily* No, no, no. I was saying that, under the guidance of the committee, the members of each of these societies would organise themselves to work the combined farms on a large scale by up-to-date methods. And I believe that, in a few years, there would be twice as good crops, in quality as well as in quantity –

RAB: *looking up from* Budget, *and laughing* God, but these divorce cases are the gran' value!

SAM: Is there another o' them this week?

RAB: Aye, half a dozen. Listen to this, 'Sensational divorce scandal. The co-respondent cross examined. Startlin' rivilations. Damin' ividence of his mother-in-law. The verdic'. A exceptional interestin' case o' divorce came up today before his honour the judge' –

JAMES: *angrily* For heaven's sake, Rab, keep quiet. Read your morbid literature if you want to, but don't interrupt when anyone is speaking.

RAB: *surprised* Oh, weel, whatever ye say.

SAM: Ach, wait a minute, Jamie; wait till we hear –

FATHER: Sam, hae some manners, and listen to your brother. It's no every day he's here. Ye can read the divorce case afther.

SAM: Oh weel, g'on then, Jamie.

JAMES: *very annoyed* Let me see. Where was I?

Father and Sam shake their heads blankly.

JAMES: Doesn't matter. I think I have explained the main points of the idea to you. What do you think of it?

FATHER: *cautiously* Weel – I don't know – just at the minute. I wud need to think it over a bit. I'm – I'm no sure abot it, Jamie.

Rab, reading, laughs aloud. Sam turns and asks him what it is about.

JAMES: But I am sure about it, Father. I intend to call a meeting of the countryside and lay the scheme before them.

FATHER: A meetin'?

SAM: In the Orange Hall?

JAMES: No, no. It can't be in the Orange Hall.

FATHER: But the's no other hall hereabouts.

JAMES: You see, it wouldn't do to have it there. We want everybody into this. Neither the Home Rulers nor Catholics would come to it. I'll hold it in the big meadow.

SAM: Home Rulers in it?

AUNT: *throwing down the* Christian Herald An' Catholics? Lord a Mercy!

FATHER: Jamie lad, I doubt – doubt –

AUNT: A meeting of Home Rulers in our meadow. Lord a mercy!

JAMES: *exasperated* Oh how long is this damnable division of the people to last? This miserable suspicion?

RAB: *reaching over the* Budget *to Sam* It's dam good this week. The's three murders in it. *Rising and stretching himself* I'll ha'e to go an' cut them turmits.

Goes out. Sam buries himself in the Budget, *Aunt is reading* Christian Herald, *Father begins to doze in his chair.*

JAMES: But I will carry it through. I will bring all creeds and classes together on a common platform, and allow them to learn by practical experience that –

He stops, seeing the no-one is listening. Sam, reading, chuckles to himself, Father snores.

JAMES: I am alone in this.

He rises and looks around him for a moment. Then goes and takes down his hat.

SAM: *looking up from his paper* Are ye going out, Jamie? *Goes on reading.*

AUNT: The partritch'll be ready in half an hour.

Goes on reading. Father still asleep. James puts on his hat and goes out slowly, without speaking.

Scene Two

The same place a week later. Aunt Margaret is discovered sweeping the floor

AUNT: The very mischief wudn't keep this floor clean wi' trampin' in an' out that goes on. Ach, a wuman's work is never done.

She puts down brush and goes into room left. James enters. He is hatless and dishevelled. He looks quickly around kitchen; then goes into room right. Aunt comes out carrying knives. She takes down the knife board and begins to clean them.

AUNT: *looking at the clock* Five o'clock. The meetin'll be goin on now in the meadow. I wonder how they're taking it? Ach, they'll jist laugh at him. They'll see he's mad, and they'll no bother their heeds.

Rab comes in laughing.

AUNT: Is the meeting ower already?

RAB: Aye.

AUNT: An' what way did it go?

RAB: Oh it was a gran' meetin'. I niver seen a better fight.

AUNT: Glory be! A fight?

RAB: Aye, better nor any twelfth.

AUNT: Is that a cut ye hae on your cheek?

RAB: *feeling with one finger* Ach, it only a scrab. It was worth it.

AUNT: An whut started it?

RAB: Och nothin'. It just started itself, like any other fight, afor anybody knowed.

AUNT: *philosophically* An' when you think of it, whut else cud ye expect but a fight, bringin' Home Rulers an' Catholics, an' Dippers, and Tramps, an a the riff-raff o' the country into the same field? It's flyin' in the face o' providence.

RAB: That's what it is, in sowl!

AUNT: It just answers him rightly. Wuz the' much speechifying?

RAB: Aye, a good deal o't – as far as I mind. Jamie started the show of course. He blethered away in that high-falutin' style o' his striking a heroic posture for near han' an hour. To tell ye the truth, I'm no sure whut it was all about, for I wuz crackin' the whole time to a wheen o' girls. *Laughs* Lizzie Kilpatrick wuz yin o' them. She's a dam fine lass, thon. *Coming closer to Aunt* Ye know – I hae my eye on Lizzie this good while.

AUNT: Och, I'm tired listenin' to your talk about Lizzie Kilpatrick. Whut about the speeches?

RAB: Oh aye – Weel, as I say, I wasn't botherin' my heed much, at the start, but as far as I mind, about half a dozen got up in turns an' said as it might be a good thing and it might be not, they had no knowins. Then Andy Moore got up – no young Andy, the oul' man – an' he said they were goin' till upset the Crown and Constitution. An at the wind up he axed Jamie if he could gie scripture for it, an Jamie as much as said he cudn't. Then somebody shouted 'Socialism', and Ned Graham – he wuz drunk – he shouted it was a Fenian thing, an' he kep' shoutin' that the whole time. An sez I to myself, this is goin' to be the warm meetin'.

Rab goes towards the door and meets Sam coming in. His clothes bear evidence of the fight.

RAB: *coming in again* Hallo, any bones broke?

SAM: No, I wasn't much in the fight. I wuz only tryin' to keep them off Jamie.

AUNT: *anxiously* Where did he go?

SAM: Oh, I don't know. He slipped off in the middle o' the rumpus.

AUNT: Huh, it'll be a lesson to him. An' what happened afther that, Rab?

RAB: *thinking* Afther that the' wuz somebody got up and spouted – *looking to Sam for confirmation* – about machinery.

SAM: Aye, that wuz Hughey Gibb – no' oul' Hughey – Mary's man.

RAB: The very boy!

SAM: He said if they were goin' to bring in a' sorts o' machinery for to do the work, whut wuz goin' to become of the poor laborours? 'The's little enough work for them as it is,' says he.

AUNT: An' goodness knows but he's right. An' what then?

RAB: *laughing* Oh afther that the' wuz no more speechifying. The first thing I knowed wuz Ned Graham getting a judases in the face. The poor fella wuz drunk – how did he know what he wuz shoutin'?

Aunt holds up her hands appealingly.

SAM: *indignantly* Who hut him?

RAB: I cudn't say for sure. But *threateningly* we'll find out. Then the fun started. Yin tuk this side, and yin tuk that – I tuk Ned's. An' afore ye cud say tea-totem the' wuz a holy war goin' on. Och it wuz the grandest fights iver wuz seen in the country side!

SAM: Man, it wuz that. D'ye know, I half expected the' wud be a toss up.

RAB: Ach, sure that's what iverbody went for. Did you think it wuz to listen to those speeches?

SAM: *regretfully* I hadn't half a chance. I had to look afther that brother of mine.

AUNT: Weel, weel, it a lesson till him. Maybe he'll hae some sense afther this. *Suddenly remembering herself* Dear a dear, look at me standin' here as if I had nothing to do! *She goes out by door at back.*

SAM: The boys are away to bring out the drums.

RAB: B'heavens, they'll be some stir yet maybe. It wud be a good chance to light the tar barrels, eh?

SAM: Aye, it wud that.

RAB: We'll do it. *Confidentially and coming close to Sam* Sam, I'll be drunk tonight.

SAM: I wudn't argue.

RAB: *sadly* Aye, but this'll be the wind up – the very last.

Sam laughs sceptically.

RAB: Ye may laugh, Sam, but it's no joke this time. Listen, I spoke the word to Lizzie Kilpatrick the day –

SAM: Aye.

RAB: An' it's a bargain, Sam – if I sign the pledge again Sunday.

SAM: *astonished* Sign the pledge! But sure man, ye're no goin' to dae that?

RAB: *hopelessly* The's nothing else for it.

SAM: I wudn't sign the pledge for no wuman.

RAB: Ah, but you were never in love, Sam.

SAM: How do you know? *Boastingly* Weel, I wuz. But axin a fella to sign the pledge! That's goin ower far. Just think Rab, a the harvest time when the sun's swetin' down on ye', an' somebody brings a bucket o' porter up till the field, an' you havin' to drink buttermilk or somethin'. It's agin nature.

RAB: Aye, it's no fair, it's no fair. *Pause* But a' the same, she's a fine girl, Lizzie.

SAM: Ye'll rue it man, ye'll rue it.

RAB: I'll chance it.

SAM: I'm telling ye, many's a time ye'll be sorely bothered for a drink.

RAB: I'll chance it. *Goes to the door and then looks back* But, maybe I'll no be able to keep it very long. *Goes out.*

SAM: *sits thinking for a moment, then laughs* Oh aye.

Aunt comes in.

AUNT: An' there be a lesson for you, Sam McKinstry –

SAM: *thoughtfully* Aye, Rab's a fool.

AUNT: Eh?

SAM: *sitting up* Whut kind o' lesson d'ye mean?

AUNT: No to be readin' books an' fillin' your heed wi' trash an' rubbish o' ivery sort, an' makin' a fool o' yourself an' a' your family like your brother Jamie there.

Sam rises and walks to the door.

SAM: *with decision* Oh, no fears o' that eather. *He stands a moment looking out.* Here's the oul' man an' Minnie along wi' him.

He goes off. Minnie stops him outside, and is seen through the window talking anxiously to him. Father comes in, looking very angry.

AUNT: Weel, William John McKinstry, whut d'ye think o' the great meeting? An' the wonderful things your son Jamie wuz goin' to do? Did I no' tell ye he wuz mad? Did I no' warn ye, to the bat o' the stick, whut wud happen? *Resignedly* But theses days an oul' women's words count for nothing!

FATHER: *impatiently* Oh for god's sake stap talkin' about it! I'm disgraced! I'll never be able to luck my neighbours in the face again! *Goes to room left. Minnie enters excited and alarmed.*

MINNIE: Och, where is he at all? Sam doesn't know. Nobody knows. If they find him they'll kill him, sure.

AUNT: *reassuringly* Na, they'll no bother their heeds ony mair. They'll just forget about him.

Father comes from room and sits by the fire, talking to himself morosely.

MINNIE: *to Father* Oh, wasn't it awful at the field?

FATHER: Not a word about it, girl. No' a word.

Minnie starts back. She sits down by the table and rests her head on her hands.

AUNT: *to Minnie* I'll get the tay. You narves is upset – wan' no wonder. A cup o' tay'll do ye nae harm.

Aunt goes out and returns carrying a bucket of water which she empties in the kettle, and sets it upon the fire.

FATHER: *to himself, while Aunt is out* I'm ruined. I'll niver be able to houl' my heed up again. An' me an elder in the church an', an' – oh God!

Aunt is busy at the fire. Father is sitting in armchair thinking, and Minnie sitting beside the table. The room door right opens softly, and James enters. Minnie rises quickly and runs over to him. The other turn round and look at him.

MINNIE: James! *He draws himself away from her, but holds her hand.*

AUNT: *coming from fire* Oh, so you're back are ye? Ye may thank your lucky stars it's wi' a whole skin.

JAMES: *sitting down beside his father* Father –

FATHER: *holding up his hand for silence* Boy, no tryin' to make excuses! The's no excuse for ye! I'm disgraced! They'll think I wuz tryin' to help ye wi' your nonsense! *Rising angrily* Luk here, why the divil did ye not tell me afore whut kind of thing it wuz? How wuz I to know ye were goin' to bring down the whole country side on the top o' my heed? *In disgust* You're a boy!

JAMES: But, Father, I did. I tried to tell you a dozen times.

FATHER: Thried? Thried, did ye? Why did ye' no' tell it to me in plain language? How wuz I to make sense of your high-falutin' talk? *Solemnly* Listen to me, Jamie; if ye try ony mair o' this lunatic work I'll wash my han's o' ye', I wull.

JAMES: *laughing cheerfully* Have no fears of that, Father. There will be no more of it. I have learned my lesson.

AUNT: *clasping he hands* Thank the Lord!

MINNIE: Oh, I am so glad!

FATHER: *looks at him a moment, sceptically* Weel, I'm pleased to hear it, Jamie. But – I'm doubtfu' if ye'll be able to keep long out o' trouble o' some sort.

AUNT: Wi' his heed fu' o sich mad notions –

FATHER: *signalling to Aunt to be silent* Howaniver, we'll say nae mair aboot it. We were a' young and foolish yin time. Jamie'll get sense like the rest o' us.

MINNIE: *coming over to him* Oh, he has learned sense already. Haven't you dear?

James nods his head meditatively but does not speak

FATHER: *rising* I wonder if them horses wuz wathered?

He goes out. Aunt goes into room left and is heard laying the table. Minnie sits down beside James. He sits looking gloomily into the fire.

MINNIE: Oh dear, you're bad company, sir. Why do you not talk to me?

JAMES: *wearily* Eh? What is there to talk about? *To himself* Ah, it was horrible, it was terrible. And to think they are so blind that they lose sight of their true interested and stone their friends for the sake of a meaningless catchword!

MINNIE: Don't bother about them, dear. I see nothing the matter with them. *Another silence* Oh well, don't talk to me then. Just as you please.

AUNT: *off, from room* Minnie, is the kettle near boiling?

MINNIE: Very near.

AUNT: Set the tay pot on the hob to warm.

Minnie does so.

JAMES: *sitting up suddenly in chair* Yes, I have done with them. I have done with them. You get no thanks for trying to help other people. Some philosopher said that long ago, and it is true yet. From this onward I work for myself. *Minnie nods delightedly and takes his hand.* Grand noble ideas are aright in books, but not in real life; I am disillusioned, Minnie. So far as I am concerned, they can go to –

MINNIE: *holding up her finger* Hush! *Aunt has come out of room during this speech.*

AUNT: Now that's sense, James McKinstry. That's the first sensible word I hae heard out o' your mouth since ye came hame. *She takes knives from drawer and goes back into room.*

MINNIE: Oh, I knew right well you'd come round, dear. *Love business* And you will go with me to the bazaar, won't you? *James nods.* And the races? *Nods* And the picnic? *Nods* And you'll drive me about as usual – and – and – make love to me? *Love business.*

JAMES: Of course, silly. *Aunt enters and looks at them a moment unseen.*

AUNT: There now, that's liker the thing! *Minnie draws herself away quickly* Minnie, put a match to the lamp the tay's ready. *She goes to outside door and calls* Come in for your tay, d'ye hear? Is that you, Sam?

SAM: *off, distant* Aye.

AUNT: Tell them to come in for their tay.

FATHER: I'll hae to see the coo doctor about that calf.

Sam and Rab come in with wet hands and dry them on the rolling towel behind the door.

RAB: Man, the'll be gran stir the night.

SAM: Aye, the half o' them's drunk a'ready.

FATHER: *severely* Rab, nae drinking. Mind whut I say.

RAB: *carelessly* Aye.

FATHER: If ye come hame dhrunk the night ye may take your notice.

RAB: Aye.

FATHER: Ye got warnings enough.

RAB: Aye.

AUNT: *taking teapot from hob and holding her apron below it* Come up. Come up, all o' ye. Sam, bring that ither lamp. *Sam takes it down. All rise except James, and go in the room. Minnie lingers at door waiting*

MINNIE: Come on, James.

He does no answer but sits looking into fire. Minnie sits down again. Father appears in doorway.

FATHER: Come up, Jamie.

JAMES: *despondently* No, I couldn't eat. Let me sit here. Go on, Minnie and get your tea.

They look at him a moment curiously, then they also go into room. The stage is dark except for the fire, and the light which comes through room door. There is a clatter of cups and sound of talking. Rab is heard laughing loudly now and then.

James sits in the arm chair facing the fire. He lies back sometime silently. Then he laughs to himself.

JAMES: A nice ending to all my dreams! *Pause* I wonder if I could have done anything? Was it an accidental failure? The first attempt is often a failure, that's a fact. *Sitting up suddenly* God! I wonder if I am a coward for giving in my gun at the first reverse? *Pause* I might carry it out yet – in spite of everything. *Sinking back* I might – I might – I might.

There is the sound of distant cheering and then of drums. James starts and sits up straight listening intently.

JAMES: *slowly* Listen!

A pause. Then the sound of talking becomes louder in the room, and Rab laughs loudly. Then silence except for the distant drums.

JAMES: *sitting back slowly in the chair* No... No...

Curtain

SAM M'KINSTRY.

"I would'nt sign the pledge for no woman."

Programme of the first performance of *The Enthusiast* and the season of 1904-05 performed by the Ulster Literary Theatre.

ULSTER LITERARY THEATRE. . . . .

The aim of this Society is to produce literary and artistic plays, and to encourage in Ulster a school of writers and actors of such plays. Those who are interested in the development of a native and local dramatic art are invited to become members or subscribers.

The Secretary,
Ulster Literary Theatre.
109 Donegall Street, Belfast.

ULAD. . . . .

The organ of the Ulster Literary Theatre. The second number will be on sale in the Hall. It can also be obtained from any Bookseller, or direct from W. Erskine Mayne, 3 Donegall Square W., Belfast. Price Sixpence.

SAMHAIN, AN OCCASIONAL REVIEW, EDITED BY Mr. W. B. YEATS. . . . .

The new number contains a detailed exposition of the aims and methods of the Irish National Theatre Society, by the Editor, and Plays by Lady Gregory and by Mr. J. M. Synge, and Miss A. E. Horniman's Letter to the Society offering it the free use of the Abbey Theatre, Dublin. Samhain is published by Messrs. Sealy, Bryers and Walker, Middle Abbey Street, Dublin, and sold by all Booksellers. Price One Shilling.

ULSTER . . LITERARY THEATRE.

Season 1904-5

PROGRAMME ONE PENNY

Davidson & M'Cormack, Printers, 54 King Street, Belfast.

THE ENTHUSIAST. . . . A COMEDY IN TWO SCENES, BY LEWIS PURCELL. . . . . . .

People of the Play:

WILLIAM JOHN M·KINSTRY	A Farmer
JAMES M·KINSTRY	His Son, home from Belfast on vacation
SAM M·KINSTRY	Brother of James
AUNT MARGET	Housekeeper to her Brother
MINNIE	Engaged to James
RAB	A Servant Man

SCENE I—A Farm Kitchen in the southern portion of the County Antrim.

SCENE II—The same, a week later.

The Present Day.

MUSIC:

Gavotte — Bach.

(a) Allemande
(b) Cebell — Henry Purcell (1658-1695).

Is breágh an cailín í. A reverie on "The Lark in the Clear Air," specially written for this production by C. G. Hardebeck.

Dirge. Specially written for this production by Uilliam Donn.

THE LITTLE COWHERD OF SLAINGE. . . A DRAMATIC LEGEND IN TWO SCENES, BY SEOSAMH MAC CATHMHAOIL. . . . .

People of the Legend:

ROS RUADH	The Red King of Crioch Slainge
FIONNGHUALA	His Daughter
EITHNE	Fostermother to Fionnghuala
AODH	A Noble Youth, at foster with Ros
FERGHAL	A Dogboy
SEANCHAN	A Man of Knowledge

Bearers, Mourning-Women, etc.

SCENE I—Morning. The Playing Green, outside the King's hunting booth, on the shore by Carlingford Lough.

SCENE II—Night, on Cnoc-na-Leaba, the Hill of Graves.

About 500 A.D.

During the interval between the plays, Songs by Messrs. Fred Hughes, R. M. Patterson, and Cahal O'Byrne. . . . .

String Band, led by Mr. T. J. Lindsay.

The Scenery by Mr. Fred Morrow.

An Introduction to Thompson in Tir-na-nOg

by **John McCann**
Outreach Director of Tinderbox Theatre Company

'He hated cruelty in any shape or form and the cruelty of bigotry – of lack of thought for things beautiful; the cruelty of extremists who hammered on dogmas, or drums, or on human beings.'

Rutherford Mayne speaking of Gerald MacNamara.

In 2001 I was asked by Ophelia Byrne, then Performing Arts Archivist at the Linen Hall Library, to work as Outreach Officer on the *State of Play?* exhibition. A significant challenge lay in deciding which plays where to be included in the exhibition and publication, reducing long-list to final selection. This process of selection also informed which plays would become the raw material and stimuli for accompanying outreach workshops. Happily, the chosen works included a short, one-act play that I had only heard fond mention of on the amateur theatre circuit. This was my first introduction to *Thompson in Tir-na-nOg* by Gerald MacNamara. What I became properly acquainted with during *State of Play?* was a much neglected gem of a play whose intense appeal during previous decades became abundantly clear.

The accompanying outreach workshops, held in schools across Northern Ireland, were designed to promote an awareness of, as Ophelia Byrne notes in her introduction to the exhibition publication, 'a 'line' of theatre works throughout the twentieth century which have been of both cultural and theatrical significance to their immediate society in Ulster'. *State of Play?* provided a valuable opportunity to explore with young people the realities of their lived experience against the backdrop of life in Ulster explored by a century of playwriting and performance. Participants aged between 15 and

18 years creatively addressed issues such as identity, stereotyping, language, cultural imagery and iconography as understood and experienced by them, and against this discovered how the same issues were presented on the Ulster stage by our playwrights.

At one stage in the workshop process selected extracts from key plays were read. Participants were then asked in what context these words might have been spoken and, more precisely, at what point during the past hundred years might these words have been said. The workshops were not a history lesson. All the information contained within the text was mined; use of language, character names, play title and stage directions. The prevalent feeling was that phrases and sentiments spoken by characters flowing from the pens of MacNamara to McGuinness, from Carnduff to Parker, have a strong if not overwhelming contemporary relevance. For young people in 2001 it was as though the ink was still wet on the century-old playwright's page.

A vital function of new writing for the theatre is to record the cultural DNA of a people at a certain point in time. A number of workshop participants saw the prevailing relevancy of one hundred years of drama reflecting a troubled and divided society as somewhat of an indictment upon our community. Have the grassroots concerns of generations of Ulster men and women as represented on stage really remained so unchanged? All plays are new plays at one point in time, but some plays remain more 'new' than others. What *Thompson in Tir-na-nOg* helped hundreds of schoolchildren discover was that it might take another hundred years before the contemporary shine has left certain *State of Play?* works.

Many local writers and actors will mark as having an inspirational affect upon them the first time they attended the theatre and heard a local dialect flowing from the mouths of recognisable characters that inhabit the stage. In this moment is the realisation that we possess stories deserving of dramatic expression, that we can hold a mirror to ourselves in an attempt to address issues that are of immediate concern. On a fundamental level, it is the acknowledgement and celebration of a cultural richness. In this light, our protagonist Thompson is a character with which few of us will claim to be unfamiliar.

The political backdrop provided to Thompson's first staging was the signing of the Ulster Covenant only four months previously. The political climate, specifically unionist opposition towards Home Rule, had created a population highly sensitive to real or perceived threats from whatever quarter in late 1912. The very act of writing, let alone staging, this play was undoubtedly a risk. And so, in the days prior to opening night at the Grand Opera House rumourmongers had created the notion that *Thompson in Tir-na-nOg* was to be openly 'anti-Orange' and generally offensive to Protestant culture. A section of the audience had arrived at the theatre with nuts and bolts lining their pockets, anticipating the rumoured bias. The theatre management that December night in 1912 was duly worried. However, the laughter that greeted Thompson on its opening night may well indicate that much of the true significance of the play had gone unnoticed. One critic suggested that a favourable reception had been guaranteed by the staging of Rutherford Mayne's *The Drone* immediately before Thompson. Another noted MacNamara's even-handed use of parody, no one community faring worse than the other. The culture-shock experienced by his characters contains a multitude of subtleties that, if fully grasped that opening night in December 1912, could well have heralded salvos of bolts upon the Grand Opera House stage. Critics referred to the obvious similarities between the Yeatsian dramatic voice and MacNamara's dialogue. Thompson is part celebration part lambaste of this style. The court formality in Tir-na-nOg is shattered when Thompson's very presence is felt; there is a disturbance in the Gaelic force. MacNamara is mining a rich seam of contradiction, hypocrisy, misinterpretation and misinformation that would keep his fellow countrymen occupied for the next century at least, playwrights and politicians alike.

A number of years prior to Thompson's staging, a meeting in Dublin between the Irish Literary Theatre and the founders of what was to become the Ulster Literary Theatre was to be a vital catalyst. When Bulmer Hobson, during the return train journey to Belfast after meeting an 'aloof' W.B. reputedly uttered in frustration the words, 'Damn Yeats, we'll write our own plays', he was planting an angry and determined seed. With Thompson MacNamara is himself indulging in a little damning of Yeats.

Yeatsian characters are shown in a state of confusion and great flux. Gaelic poetry is replaced by an unrecognisable tongue bringing dark skies and a set of comic circumstances that dramatically enshrine Hobson's outburst.

What Thompson represents is a daring challenge to its audience, be it 1912 or 2012. Do not be lulled by the humour as we are told some original audience members were. Beneath the surface is a complex examination of many cultural strands struggling to exist in the same space. Having read the play, consider how recently Cuchulain has appeared on loyalist murals as a champion/guardian of Ulster. Does this signify two fingers to the other side of the peace-line or an attempt to redefine a tradition? Like the writing on many gable walls, the stages of Ulster over the past hundred years have chronicled where myth and reality blur. Thankfully MacNamara was just as bold in his willingness to tackle 'the cruelty of extremists who hammered on dogmas, or drums, or on human beings' as many gable artists are in their choice of colour.

Suzanne and the Sovereigns, a play jointly written by Gerald MacNamara and Lewis Purcell, first performed in December 1907.

ULSTER LITERARY THEATRE.

BROADSHEET OF THE PLAY.

SUZANNE AND THE SOVEREIGNS:

AN EXTRAVAGANZA

BY LEWIS PURCELL AND GERALD MACNAMARA.

CHARACTERS—

KING WILLIAM III., KING JAMES II., ...	Heroes.
LUNDY, ...	A Traitor.
WILHELM VAN TOOTIL,	Court Banner Painter to King William III.
SIR JOSEPH JACKSON, WILLIAM JOHN M'AULEY, FRANCY M'CANN, ...	Members of a Deputation.
DUKE SCHOMBERG, ...	of King William's Army.
ADMIRAL GINKEL, ...	of H.M.S. Disastrous.
GENERAL TYRCONNELL, COLONEL KELLY, ...	of King James' Army.
PIETE, ...	Faithful Butler to King William III.
ROBERT HAMLET M'BRIDE, ...	A Versatile Innkeeper.
CAPTAIN OF THE GUARD.	
FIRST TOWN GUARD.	
SECOND TOWN GUARD.	
CAPTAIN OF THE PACKET-BOAT, "THE HAPPY-GO-LUCKY."	
AND	
SUZANNE, ...	... A BEAUTEOUS MAID

SOLDIERS, SAILORS, CITIZENS, &c.

FIRST ACT.

SCENE I.—The Audience Chamber of the Stadhuis, at Amsterdam.

SCENE II.—On board the Packet-boat, "The Happy-Go-Lucky."

SECOND ACT.

SCENE I.—Inside the Walls of Derry.

SCENE II.—King James' Camp, outside the Walls of Derry.

THIRD ACT.

SCENE I.—A Wood near Carrickfergus.

SCENE II.—The Quay at Carrickfergus.

FOURTH ACT.

"The White Horse" Inn, near the Boyne.

Three weeks are supposed to elapse between Scene I. of the First Act and Scene II. of the Third Act. The intervals between the various other Scenes and Acts may be found out from almost any good history.

Note.—The authors have attempted to write a play, not a text-book for students. But members of the audience who may be inclined to dismiss certain scenes and incidents as resting on no basis of historical fact are requested to suspend judgment until, in addition to the works of popular authors like Macaulay, Lecky, Froude and Leland, they have carefully studied and collated the undermentioned authorities:—

"Journals of the House of Commons of Ireland, 1613-1800" (19 vols. folio);
"Journals of the Irish House of Lords" (18 vols.).
"Ninth Report of the Deputy Keeper of Public Records, Ireland" (Dublin, 1877).
Cane's "History of Williamite and Jacobite Wars in Ireland."
"Collectanea de rebus Hibernicis."
"Essai Historique sur l' Irlande."
Mackenzie's "Narrative of the Siege of Derry."
Howell's "State Trials" (15 vols.).
"Memoires de Madame de la Fayette."
"Faithful History of the Northern Affairs of Ireland from King James' Accession to the Siege of Londonderry" (Dublin, 1690).
Zeuss' "Grammatica Celtica."
"Ceachta beaga Gaedhilge."
"Irish Auxiliary of the London Society for Promoting Christianity among the Jews; third annual report" (Dublin, 1821).

DAVIDSON & M'CORMACK, PRINTERS, BELFAST.

The Ulster Literary Theatre on Tour.

Thompson in Tir-na-nOg

Gerald MacNamara (1865-1938) was the pen name of Harry C. Morrow. Born into a liberal, artistic and intellectual family from Comber, Co. Down, he was both a playwright and a gifted actor. Eleven of his comedies were performed by the Ulster Literary Theatre, including *The Mist That Does Be on The Bog* (1909), a parody of Synge, *Suzanne and the Sovereigns* (1907), a historical burlesque co-written with David Parkhill and the following play. Little personal information exists about his life. His death coincided with the end of the Ulster Literary Theatre as an independent force in Northern Irish theatre.

Thompson in Tir-na-nOg (1912)

A play in one act

By Gerald MacNamara

PEOPLE OF THE PLAY

High King of Tir-na-nOg
Finn
Angus
Cuchulain of the Ford
Conan Macmorna
Maev
Grania
Thompson of Scarva

SCENE

The private grounds of the High King of Tir-na-nOg.

First produced in the Grand Opera House, Belfast, 9th December, 1912 by members of the Ulster Literary Theatre.

KING: *seated centre* What has befallen our land this day, this land of eternal youth and happiness – beloved Tir-na-nOg. O sad is my heart, and my tongue is troubled with speaking in this new and curious language. Can it be that the knowledge of the Gaelic has utterly forsaken me, or is it but an evil spell which soon may pass away?

Enter Finn.

FINN: *making a low bow* Greetings to thee, O king of Tir-na-nOg.

KING: *bowing. Aside* Poor Finn, he's got it too.

FINN: O King, I am in dire distress; I have been stricken with a malady which troubles me to understand. I have lost all words of Gaelic, and in their stead I speak this language which must sound curious to thine ears.

King shakes his head.

Ah! I see 'tis useless to address the King in such a barbarous language. *Turns to go off left.*

KING: In truth I do, but much against my will. What can be its portent?

FINN: Methinks it is an evil spell.

KING: O fickle Finn, hast though so soon forgotten? Remember we are still in Tir-na-nOg, which thou and I and others here have won by faithfulness and valour in the ancient land of Erin.

FINN: Yet spell it must be, for the feeling in my bones reminds me of the spells which Angus of the Danaan people was wont to put on us.

KING: I do remember well those spells, yet Angus lodges in our peaceful land today, and none can say that he has practised these black arts of late.

FINN: 'Tis troth, but thou canst never tell.

Enter Angus left.

ANGUS: *bowing* Greetings to the High King of Tir-na-nOg, and to thee, O Finn, Ardrie of Benmadigan and ruler of the lands around Ardglass.

KING: You also speak in this strange tongue. Where has thy Gaelic gone?

ANGUS: O King, for reasons I was forced to exercise my power of casting spells.

FINN: I told you so.

KING: I hope you have good reason as you will shortly know.

FINN: But what language is it that you've put upon us?

ANGUS: I ordered purest English.

KING: English! What people are the English?

ANGUS: They hail from the land beyond the Eastern Sea.

KING: What! Those barbarians! A people who were wont to paint their bodies red and white and blue.

FINN: And who, we're told, did eat their near relations.

ANGUS: From what I hear, they're much improved of late.

KING: But what is all beside the case – why put this English on us? We like it not; we much prefer our Gaelic.

ANGUS: I own the feeling is most natural, but still I would have you understand that English now is spoken throughout our natal land.

KING: When did these tidings reach you?

ANGUS: This morn at sunrise I did meet a strange young man from Erinn?

KING & FINN: *together* From Erinn?

KING: And his name?

ANGUS: His name is Thompson.

Thunder and lightning

KING: Angus, what meaneth this?

ANGUS: I know not, save that it be the mention of the name of Thompson.

KING: I've never known such name in Erinn.

FINN: Most like he is a son of Thomp.

KING: I have no doubt, but who the – who is Thomp?

ANGUS: I know not, saving that he hails from Erinn.

KING: How comes he here in Tir-na-nOg, where none has come for many thousand moons?

ANGUS: 'Tis very strange, but let me tell my story.

KING: Proceed and make it brief.

ANGUS: This morning, as I fed my birds of knowledge in my garden, I espied a stranger. His garments were most strange, and his features were much stranger. I approached him and addresses him thus.

KING: In English?

ANGUS: No, in Gaelic, for I knew no other tongue just then. I said *Ceud mile failte.* At this he was most pleased but answered me in English.

KING: And did you understand?

ANGUS: I did not, for to me it sounded like the bark of dogs. I was sore distressed, for I was anxious to have converse with him. I then recalled to my mind my powers in ancient days of casting spells, so I tried to throw the Gaelic tongue upon him.

KING: And did your spell not give entire satisfaction?

ANGUS: An utter failure.

FINN: 'Tis strange, for your great spells were never known to fail.

ANGUS: It was not that he could not speak the Gaelic. 'Twas that he would not.

KING: And does he say that he is of Irish birth?

ANGUS: He voweth so. He says he comes from Scarva.

KING: Tell us more of this strange man from Scarva.

ANGUS: As I could not make him speak in Gaelic, I threw a spell upon myself and spoke to him in English.

KING: How comes it that you cast a spell on us as well?

ANGUS: And this, O King, is how it is – when I first spoke in English, I explained the nature of our country. How it was the land of youth and peace, and how I wished to bring him to our King and give him royal welcome.

KING: *impatiently* Bring Thompson forth, why keep him lingering at our royal gates? I long to see him.

ANGUS: Alas, it cannot be.

KING: For why?

ANGUS: Because he ran away.

KING & FINN: *together* He ran away!

ANGUS: Yes, fleet as forest deer, and as he ran he shouted loud, 'It's an asylum!'

KING: His conduct is most strange.

ANGUS: And this is how it was. I put an English spell on everyone in Tir-na-nOg, that all might speak with him and make him feel at home.

KING: Angus, thou hast always been most famous for thy wisdom. Come let us go in search of Thompson.

Enter Cuchulain and Conan.

CONAN: *excitedly* O High King of Tir-na-nOg, thy people are in deep distress, for they have lost their Gaelic.

KING: Fear not, O Conan, all will soon be well, and thou, Cuchulain, do not tremble, for thy Gaelic words will soon come back again.

CUCHULAIN: I tremble not, O King; I have no fear, nor ever had I.

KING: *patting him on the back* I know, I know.

CUCHULAIN: 'Twas not much Gaelic that I ever spoke; my sword spoke for me.

KING: Well said, Cuchulain, thy words are like a saga.

CONAN: *trembling* But why this strange departure from our ancient usage?

KING: 'Twas Angus here who gave us power to speak like this.

CONAN: But we dislike it.

KING: Yes, yes, I know, but this was done that all might speak with Thompson who is a stranger.

CUCHULAIN: A stranger! This is something new in Tir-na-nOg.

KING: Come, let us not delay. *To Cuchulain and Conan* We go in search of Thompson.

Exit King, Finn and Angus left.

CONAN: This Thompson man must surely be a warrior brave from Erinn.

CUCHULAIN: What makes you say so, Conan?

CONAN: No man comes here to Tir-na-nOg who has not done great deeds in battle.

CUCHULAIN: How comes it that you are here, O Conan?

CONAN: Have I not done great deeds?

CUCHULAIN: Thy greatest was with the Liagan.

CONAN: Did I not cut his head clean off?

CUCHULAIN: No doubt, but still it was a foul.

CONAN: All's fair in war.

CUCHULAIN: But that was most unfair. I'm told when Liagan's sword was oe'er your head, in fear you called out mockingly 'Truly thou art in more peril from the man behind you than in front.' Liagan looked round and instantly you swept his head clean off and ran away.

CONAN: 'Twas but a jest.

CUCHULAIN: Such sorry jests do not become a follower of Finn.

CONAN: What know you of Finn? You who belong to another cycle?

CUCHULAIN: Have I not heard from Finn's own lips, how he did strike with one great blow three prince's heads off?

CONAN: That was a blow.

CUCHULAIN: You doubt his word! I'd rather have the word of Finn than coward's bonds like thine.

CONAN: You call me coward, you who ran away from Ferdia at the Ford.

CUCHULAIN: I – I ran from Ferdia at the Ford? *Threateningly* Say that once more and I will make two halves of you.

Enter Queen Maev and Grania.

CUCHULAIN: O Maev, Queen of Connacht, fairest of all women, bear me witness, did I not hold the Ford 'gainst Ferdia?

QUEEN: O that thou surely didst, to my great sorrow, but who should say thee nay?

CUCHULAIN: *pointing at Conan* 'Twas he, the coward.

QUEEN: Durst doubt the word of warriors of our cycle, thou low-born third cyclarian?

GRANIA: *to Queen* Put no reproach upon my people. Our cycle is as good as thine. Our records of great deeds are not as numerous as thine, but ours are at least true.

QUEEN: How durst thou so address a Queen in whose veins flow the blood of the gods. How durst thou, hussy!

Enter King, Angus and Finn.

KING: My children! My children! Remember this is Tir-na-nOg where all is peace and love and joy.

QUEEN: I crave thy pardon, noble King, for being thus excited.

GRANIA: Our good tempers must have left us with our lovely Gaelic tongue.

King pats Grania on the back.

CUCHULAIN: Hast thou seen aught, O King, of Thompson?

KING: The gods have smiled not on our efforts; our search was vain. *Great cheering and laughing outside.*

Enter Thompson left – excited.

KING: *looking off* They are the children of Lir. They give you welcome to the land of youth.

THOMPSON: They have a quare way of doing it.

KING: Did they say aught to give offence?

THOMPSON: They were shoutin' 'Look at the ould lad.'

KING: I'm sure 'twas not intended for offence.

Thompson attempts to exit left.

Stay, O Thompson, stay a little longer.

Thompson stops in centre of stage beside King.

We give you welcome to our land this day. *All bow* I have no doubt you have heard of us all in story.

Thompson nods his head stupidly.

And you must also know what land you stand in.

THOMPSON: Well now, mister, I couldn't just name the district, but it must be either Co. Down or Armagh.

KING: 'Tis neither one nor other – it's Tir-na-nOg.

THOMPSON: Which?

KING: It's Tir-na-nOg, and I'm its King.

THOMPSON: Just what I suspected, an asylum.

KING: We are all most anxious to discover how you left your native land.

THOMPSON: Well, the last thing I mind was yesterday about twelve o'clock. I was going to the fight at Scarva.

KING: The fight! You died in battle! It is enough. Thou has earned the just reward due to all warriors in Erinn. Although many moons have passed since last we had one worthy to approach our land, we hail thee more on that account. *All bow to Thompson.* But let me haste to introduce you to my people. This is Queen Maev, of whom no doubt you've often heard.

THOMPSON: *to King* O aye, many's the time. How long is she in?

KING: We do not go by time in Tir-na-nOg.

THOMPSON: *jokingly* All piecework. Good evening, your Majesty, I needn't ask ye how ye are, for you're lookin' brave.

QUEEN: Brave I am, and brave I ever was in the land of Erinn. There was not in Banba, nor yet in all Eire, a woman more excellent than myself. I was the most famous, the most powerful, and the best born.

THOMPSON: *cheerfully* One of the best.

QUEEN: *proudly* Not one of the best, but the best.

THOMPSON: Aye, we'll let it go at that.

QUEEN: Not even the half red Maev of Leinster was to be named beside me.

THOMPSON: Not at all, she wasn't in the same street. *Aside* The weemin' are always the worst in these places.

KING: And this is Conan.

THOMPSON: How are ye, Mister? *Attempts to shake hands.*

CONAN: *grandly* I am of the MacMornas.

THOMPSON: Just like the Scotch. Took single tickets, eh?

KING: And here is Grania, whose praises must be sung in Erinn even now.

THOMPSON: That's a fact. I'm glad to meet you, Miss. *Grania bows. Aside* I don't think she's a loony.

KING: And this is Angus.

ANGUS: My name must be familiar.

THOMPSON: O aye, I've heard the name.

ANGUS: I am of the race of the Danaan or people of the goddess Dana.

THOMPSON: *aside* This is a bad case.

ANGUS: They were a people who delighted in beauty and gaiety and fond of fine apparel.

THOMPSON: So you're one of the 'knuts'.

ANGUS: My people were skilled in magic arts, and their harpers could make music that a man who heard it would forget all earthly things.

THOMPSON: But you couldn't fit your Gaelic unto me, ye ould mesmerist. *Angus scowls.*

KING: And this is Finn the Great.

THOMPSON: *smiling* The sooner I get out of this place the better. *Is going off left when Cuchulain keeps him back.*

CUCHULAIN: If thou art a fighting man from Erinn, thou must have heard of my great deeds.

THOMPSON: What's your name, Mister?

CUCHULAIN: Cuchulain.

THOMPSON: Koo – who?

CUCHULAIN: Cuchulain.

THOMPSON: Aye, it's a fine day.

CUCHULAIN: All days are fine in Tir-na-nOg.

THOMPSON: Is that a fact? Man, we had a terrible wet summer this year.

CUCHULAIN: But hast thou never heard of Erinn?

THOMPSON: I'll tell you no lies, mister, I never did. What are you, or what were ye?

CUCHULAIN: I was of the Red Branch, foremost of the fighting men of Ulster.

THOMPSON: Ulster! Put it there. *Shakes hands* Why didn't ye tell me that before? *Brings him down stage to front and whispers* Man, I took you for a loony like the rest. *Points over his shoulder with his thumb.*

CUCHULAIN: Were you ever in Ulster?

THOMPSON: Was I ever in Ulster – was I ever in – was I ever out of it?

CUCHULAIN: I hope that Ulster still holds sway in Erinn.

THOMPSON: I dunno about holdin' sway, but she can hold her own – and more.

CUCHULAIN: I am well pleased to hear it, for I did love and still do love my Ulster. What part of Ulster have you come from?

THOMPSON: Scarva.

CUCHULAIN: Lies Scarva east or west?

THOMPSON: It's on the Great Northern.

CUCHULAIN: *reflectively* Once I was the Great Northern.

THOMPSON: *looks at Cuchulain pityingly and says aside* He's as bad as the rest, poor sowl.

CUCHULAIN: O, how I fought for Ulster. *Excitedly* When the great battle fury was on me.

THOMPSON: Now don't get excited, mister – I know what the battle fury is – I've had it often – every Twelfth – and Thirteenth.

CUCHULAIN: Whole hosts lay dead and bleeding at my feet.

THOMPSON: Now if you keep on talkin' like that they'll never let ye out.

CUCHULAIN: My skill in archery was never equalled.

THOMPSON: Now keep quiet and we'll get ye a minneture rifle.

CUCHULAIN: Alone I have routed an army.

THOMPSON: *patronisingly patting Cuchulain on the shoulder* Good man! Good man!

CUCHULAIN: As I swept into battle with my gold bronze chariot, whole nations have trembled to hear the Ulster war cry on my lips.

THOMPSON: *very excited, slapping Cuchulain on the back* True blue! Ulster will fight and Ulster will be right! *Assuming a military tone of voice* Form fours! Left urn! Quick march!

Exit left. The others on the stage look after Thompson and form in a cluster round the king.

KING: My people, I have grave doubts if this fair stranger is a worthy person for our Tir-na-nOg. He may have died in battle, but his manners please me not.

CONAN: He could never have passed the test of our Fiana.

CUCHULAIN: The Red Branch would have scorned him.

QUEEN: He comes not of a fighting brood.

GRANIA: He may have been a kern, but not a chieftain.

KING: I think that we're all agreed that Thompson's not a fit companion for our people here in Tir-na-nOg – but how are we to prove it?

ANGUS: I have a plan, High King, if you would give your royal sanction.

KING: Speak on, wise Angus.

ANGUS: I think a woman's wit would win us through this tribulation.

KING: What woman would you say?

ANGUS: I think that Grania here could wheedle out this man's confession.

KING: *turning to Grania* Are you prepared to undertake this task?

GRANIA: In truth, there's nothing I'd like better.

Thompson is heard whistling 'The Boyne Water'. *All on stage listen.*

CONAN: 'Tis Thompson, I can see him.

KING: Let us away. *To Grania* When you have discovered Thompson's history, give us a signal and we'll all return.

GRANIA: What signal should I give?

KING: If you consider him a proper person, give three barks of a dog, but if you find that he's unworthy –

GRANIA: I shall give three mews of a cat.

KING: Ssh. *Enter Thompson, very happy* We will leave you for a spell, O Thompson, till we make preparation for a royal feast in honour of your coming. Come, good people. *All leave slowly right. Grania giving the glad-eye to Thompson.*

THOMPSON: I wish you wouldn't go, Grania, for you're all right anyway.

GRANIA: *pouting* Why did you leave us with so little ceremony?

THOMPSON: Ach, I was very dry.

GRANIA: And is your thirst quite satisfied?

THOMPSON: Not quite, I only had a pint – of mead, but as the barmaid would not take the money, I couldn't out of decency ask for more.

GRANIA: *about to leave* Everything is free in Tir-na-nOg.

THOMPSON: Ach, Grania, don't be leaving me.

GRANIA: I wish to leave, yet some strange fascination holds me here.

THOMPSON: That's quare.

GRANIA: *looking at Thompson sadly* Last night I had a dream. I dreamt I saw a hero.

THOMPSON: A hero?

GRANIA: He stood like a flame against the flameless sky, and the whole sapphire of the heavens seemed to live in his fearless eyes.

THOMPSON: Well, well, did you know his face?

GRANIA: Not then, sweet Thompson.

THOMPSON: *getting closer to Grania* Have you saw him since?

GRANIA: *getting quite close to Thompson* I have today. He dwells in Tir-na-nOg.

THOMPSON: *slipping his arm round Grania's waist* Do I know him, dear? Will you give me three guesses?

GRANIA: Can you not guess in one? 'Twas none but you, O dearest Thompson. *Leans her head on his chest.*

THOMPSON: Call me Andy.

GRANIA: O Andy, Andy, my heart's desire. *They both sit on tree trunk.* Tell me, dearest, how you left old Erinn. You said you were killed in battle.

THOMPSON: I was blew up.

GRANIA: Blew up. How strange – what can be its portent?

THOMPSON: Beg pardon.

GRANIA: What does 'blew up' mean?

THOMPSON: A gun burst in my hand.

GRANIA: A gun! What is a gun?

THOMPSON: *aside* She's as bad as the rest. *To Grania* A gun – well, a gun's a gun that shoots bullets that kills people.

GRANIA: Ah, that must be a new thing.

THOMPSON: Sowl, this wasn't a new thing.

GRANIA: Where was this battle fought?

THOMPSON: In Scarva. We have one every 13th of July. Ach, it's a great sight. They come from all arts and parts to see the show. Excursion trains from Derry and Belfast. The papers used to make fun of us. Ach, but times is changed, for now the *News Letter* calls it a pageant.

GRANIA: And what part did you play in this great battle. Were you a Chieftain?

THOMPSON: I was promoted this year to be one of King William's Generals.

GRANIA: And you lead your fighting kerns into the heat of the battle?

THOMPSON: *confidently* Indeed, to tell you the truth, I never got the length of the field.

GRANIA: That is strange.

THOMPSON: I was takin' a short cut through the meadows, and while I was climbing a ditch, my ould gun burst in my hands, an' that is all I mind. I must a lay there all day and then maybe in the night I wandered about, not knowin' where I was, and then I must have fell asleep, and when I wakened up in the mornin' I didn't know where I was, and I damned if I know now – excuse me.

GRANIA: And you know not if your army was victorious or not?

THOMPSON: Sure I told you I was on King William's side. Of course we won the day.

GRANIA: Why do you say 'of course'? The fortunes of war are so uncertain.

THOMPSON: Sure, it wasn't a real fight. It was a sham fight or a pageant fight.

GRANIA: A make believe. *Thompson nods his head.*

THOMPSON: Aye, the very thing.

GRANIA: But have you been in a real fight?

THOMPSON: O aye, I was in a scrap in Portadown last Sunday.

GRANIA: And whom were you fighting in Portadown?

THOMPSON: The Hibernians.

GRANIA: *shocked* The Hiberniana! But are not all people in Erinn Hibernians?

THOMPSON: In sowl they're not.

GRANIA: Are all the people in Portadown Hiberniana?

THOMPSON: Talk sense, woman dear.

GRANIA: *looking towards audience* Many changes must have come o'er Erinn since the days of Cuchulain and Oisin. Then we were all Hibernians. *To Thompson* I wish, dearest, that you were all Hibernian too.

THOMPSON: You'll never see the day. *Rising from couch* And what's more, I'll have nothing more to do with you, for I'm no believer in mixed marriages.

GRANIA: Oh, Andy, tell me not that you fought against the Hibernians.

THOMPSON: In troth, I did! *Grania gives three mews of a cat. Aside* Ach, poor wee girl, she's the worst case of the lot. *Moves towards left.*

Enter all the others right.

KING: Secure the prisoner!

Thompson is arrested by Cuchulain and Conan.

THOMPSON: Prisoner! What do you mean?

KING: This land has always been reserved for warriors and patriots of Erinn. We consider you are neither one nor other, but by some mysterious hideous blunder you have been thrust upon us.

THOMPSON: If you let me alone I'll thrust myself out of this.

KING: That is beyond your power. Our chief desire is to give you justice, and so we will now proceed with the trial. Finn read the charge.

FINN: *unfolding parchment* Andrew Thompson, late of Scarva, Ireland, you are charged with trespass in Tir-na-nOg, you having no right, title or authority to do the same, as you have never fought, died, or done anything in the cause of the Gael. What say you Andrew Thompson – Guilty or Not Guilty?

THOMPSON: Not guilty!

FINN: Are you, Andrew Thompson, prepared to stand your trial?

THOMPSON: *trying to get away, but prevented by Cuchulain and Conan* I wish you'd let me go home.

KING: We will try you according to the ancient Brehon Laws.

THOMPSON: God help me now.

KING: Who is the first witness?

FINN: Queen Maev, my lord.

KING: Where did you see the prisoner first, my good woman?

QUEEN: On this very spot, my lord.

KING: Is the prisoner at the bar in your opinion an Irishman?

QUEEN: He is not, my lord.

THOMPSON: You're a – it's a lie – my father and mother are Irish, and I am Irish too.

KING: Why are you so convinced that this man is not Irish?

QUEEN: Because he speaks in a language foreign to Ireland.

KING: And what language do you call it?

QUEEN: It is called English.

THOMPSON: But sure you are speaking English yourself.

QUEEN: But at present we are under a spell.

Conan rises to his feet.

KING: Hast thou anything to say, brave Conan?

CONAN: I have, my lord. *To Thompson* Can you speak Irish?

THOMPSON: I can not indeed, and I don't want to.

KING: Answer the question, sir. We do not ask for your opinion.

CUCHULAIN: My lord, may I ask a few questions of the prisoner?

KING: You may.

CUCHULAIN: Andrew Thompson, do you -

THOMPSON: I object!

KING: Answer the questions, sir!

CUCHULAIN: Do you still assert that you are Irish?

THOMPSON: Of course I do.

CUCHULAIN: And you admit that you do not speak the language of your country?

THOMPSON: *proudly* The language of my country is English.

CUCHULAIN: Answer me, sir. Can you speak Irish?

THOMPSON: I told you before that I couldn't, and I –

KING: Keep silence!

CUCHULAIN: You affirm that are Irish. Are you proud of that fact?

THOMPSON: Beg pardon?

CUCHULAIN: *in a loud voice* Are you proud of your country?

THOMPSON: I am, troth.

CUCHULAIN: But as you are speaking English, any man might call you English.

THOMPSON: Would he? Well, if he did, he would never do it again.

CUCHULAIN: Why?

THOMPSON: Why? I'd break his jaw.

ANGUS: The remarks of the prisoner are most contradictory.

THOMPSON: Look here, mister, you howled yer tongue.

KING: I cannot have such language in my court.

THOMPSON: But it's not fair. Here's three solicitors for my prosecution, an' not a sowl to speak for me.

CUCHULAIN: Now, sir, assuming that thou art an Irishman.

THOMPSON: Ach, don't bother me, ye ould Quaker.

CUCHULAIN: You should at least have heard of the great deeds done by your ancestors of Ireland.

THOMPSON: And so I have.

CUCHULAIN: Let of hear something of the history of your country.

THOMPSON: Well, I know that King William won the battle of the Boyne.

CUCHULAIN: When was this battle fought.

THOMPSON: On the 12th.

CUCHULAIN: Twelfth of what?

THOMPSON: Twelfth of July, Sixteen Hundred and Ninety.

CUCHULAIN: Were you present at this battle?

THOMPSON: Ach, you're all mad.

KING: If this language continues I'll have you committed.

CUCHULAIN: If you had lived in this King's time would you have taken up arms against him?

THOMPSON: I would have fought for him tooth and nail.

CUCHULAIN: Was this William not an Irishman?

THOMPSON: He was not.

CUCHULAIN: *looking round at the Court* King William was not an Irishman. Now did this King, whom you seem to esteem so much, did he do any great deeds?

THOMPSON: Of coorse he did – he crossed the Boyne.

CUCHULAIN: He crossed the Boyne – how?

THOMPSON: On a white horse.

CUCHULAIN: Do you consider that a great deed?

THOMPSON: Of coorse I do; sure, it's painted on all the Orangemen's banners.

CUCHULAIN: Who are these Orangemen?

THOMPSON: True-born sons of William *Proudly hitting his chest* – and I am one.

CUCHULAIN: Tell us something of your father – King William.

THOMPSON: Look here, mister, I don't like to hear you talkin' in that sarcastic way about King William.

CUCHULAIN: Tell us who he was.

THOMPSON: William the Third, Prince of Orange, of glorious, pious and immortal memory, come over from Holland.

QUEEN: He was a Dutchman.

THOMPSON: I suppose he must have been. I never thought of that before, but he bate King James anyway at the battle of the Boyne.

CUCHULAIN: Who was this King James.

THOMPSON: You're very ignorant. He was the King of England, and so was King William.

KING: Both at the same time? It could not be.

THOMPSON: It's a fact – but the English people were sick of him.

KING: Sick of whom?

THOMPSON: Of King James, of coorse! Sure the English asked William to come over and reign in his place.

KING: And he consented?

THOMPSON: Sartintly – and he chased James out of England and over the water to Ireland.

CUCHULAIN: And did the Irish people welcome this England King?

THOMPSON: Of coorse they did, for he was one of their own sort.

CUCHULAIN: Do you mean he was Irish after all?

THOMPSON: Not at all.

CUCHULAIN: Then what do you mean by 'one of their own sort'?

THOMPSON: Look here, Mr. Cuckoo, I don't believe you're an Ulsterman at all.

CUCHULAIN: Do you mean to say that the Irish people had no desire for an Irish King?

THOMPSON: *looking left and making an effort to get away, but kept back by Conan* Ach, I couldn't tell you. It all happened a long while ago.

CUCHULAIN: Do you Orangemen rejoice in the victory of a foreign Prince over your own countrymen?

THOMPSON: *in a tired voice* Aye.

CUCHULAIN: And why?

THOMPSON: *angry* Because we don't want Home Rule.

CUCHULAIN: Are you too lazy to rule yourselves?

THOMPSON: Ach, it's not that, for there's heaps of them up in the South and West that want Home Rule.

CUCHULAIN: What kind of people are these?

THOMPSON: They're no class – a lot of Gaelic Leaguers and Hibernians.

CUCHULAIN: Are you not a Hibernian?

THOMPSON: If you insult me like that, I'll strike you.

CUCHULAIN: *turning to the Court* On his own word the prisoner is no Irishman.

THOMPSON: I didn't say that.

ANGUS: But the word Hibernian is the Latin form of Irishman.

THOMPSON: I know nothing about Latin, thank God.

CONAN: My lord, may I be permitted to ask a few questions?

KING: Yes, if they will lead to his conviction.

CONAN: *to Thompson* Have you ever heard of Bov the Red?

THOMPSON: *hesitatingly* I don't think I mind hearing the name.

CONAN: Or the great deeds of the Fiana?

THOMPSON: No, I don't think so.

QUEEN: Have you ever heard of Ferdia's great fight with Cuchulain at the Ford?

THOMPSON: *bored* I never did.

ANGUS: Do you know anything of the story of the Dagda?

THOMPSON: *shortly* No.

GRANIA: Have you heard of the romance of Naisi and Deirdre?

THOMPSON: I'll have nothing more to say to you, young woman.

KING: Do you know aught of your country's history save that of this Battle of the Boyne?

THOMPSON: I know that King Charles was beheaded.

KING: Was Charles an Irishman?

THOMPSON: No.

KING: What more do you know?

THOMPSON: I know that King Henry VIII was a Roman till he was converted.

CUCHULAIN: Of course he wasn't an Irishman.

THOMPSON: He was not.

KING: What has all this got to do with Ireland? We want to hear of Irish history.

THOMPSON: Shure, they never teach you Irish history in the schools of Ireland.

CUCHULAIN: It is plain, my lord, that the prisoner has no knowledge even of the great deeds performed in Ireland. Now I would like to see if he has performed any great deeds himself. *To Thompson* Did you ever fight in the cause of the Gael?

THOMPSON: The which?

CUCHULAIN: Were you in the Red Branch?

THOMPSON: No, I was in the Black Perceptory.

CUCHULAIN: Were you a Chieftain?

THOMPSON: No, I was a bleacher.

CUCHULAIN: Did you ever fight against the enemies of your country?

THOMPSON: Many's the time.

CUCHULAIN: Who were the enemies?

THOMPSON: The peelers.

FINN: Who are these peelers?

THOMPSON: Fellows that lift you.

FINN: Strong men?

THOMPSON: There's no doubt they're a fine body of men and useful sometimes for putting down them terrible atrocities in the South and the West.

CUCHULAIN: Then these peelers keep order in Ireland?

THOMPSON: They're supposed to.

KING: These peelers keep order in Ireland same as did the Fiana in our time, and you, sir, have come to Tir-na-nOg, you who have fought against the Fiana or peelers, as you now call them. It is but mockery to continue this trial any longer. I cannot condemn you to death, as such a thing as death is unknown in the land of youth, but I will put you to the test of fire. Have you anything to say?

THOMPSON: These people are mad and dangerous, Your most Gracious Majesty. If I am trespassing here it is not my fault, and you needn't blame me for knowing nothing about you and all these nice people, but anyway, sure I am doing you no harm.

KING: But you are doing us harm. You have brought with you into this land a disquieting influence; we can feel it in the air. During your short stay here you have already caused strife; even I cannot keep my temper in control.

THOMPSON: But what am I doing on you? What's wrong with me?

KING: That is beyond my ken – perhaps it is your face – but sure we are that you and we cannot exist together in this peaceful land. You must stand or perish in the test. Take him away, and build a fire around the prisoner.

THOMPSON: O, Your most Excellent Majesty, Sir Edward – King Geo – ach, I don't know what I'm talking about. Will none of you have pity on me, or stretch out a hand to save me? I'm a widow man with a large family, and my life is not insured. Your Majesty, give me a chance.

KING: It is too late.

THOMPSON: Ach, don't burn me, and I'll learn Gaelic, and I'll make the childer learn it – I will, sowl, and I have a parrot at home that my uncle brought from foreign parts; it can only whistle 'Dolly's Brae', but be heavens I'll learn it Gaelic too.

KING: Take him away, and apply the flame.

Thompson taken off shouting 'No Surrender'. *Blaze off stage.*

KING: Tell me that Thompson has departed. See that he has not left his soul behind.

FINN: There's nothing left – not even his ashes.

Thunder

KING: Then why this anger in the elements?

ANGUS: I crave your pardon, O High King. It is the English spell that is still on us.

KING: Make haste, remove it and let us have our Gaelic back again. *Holding up goblet* SLANTE!

Curtain

From left: David Parkill, Fred Morrow, Harry Morrow and Rutherford Mayne.

Bill of 1909 season by the Ulster Literary Theatre.

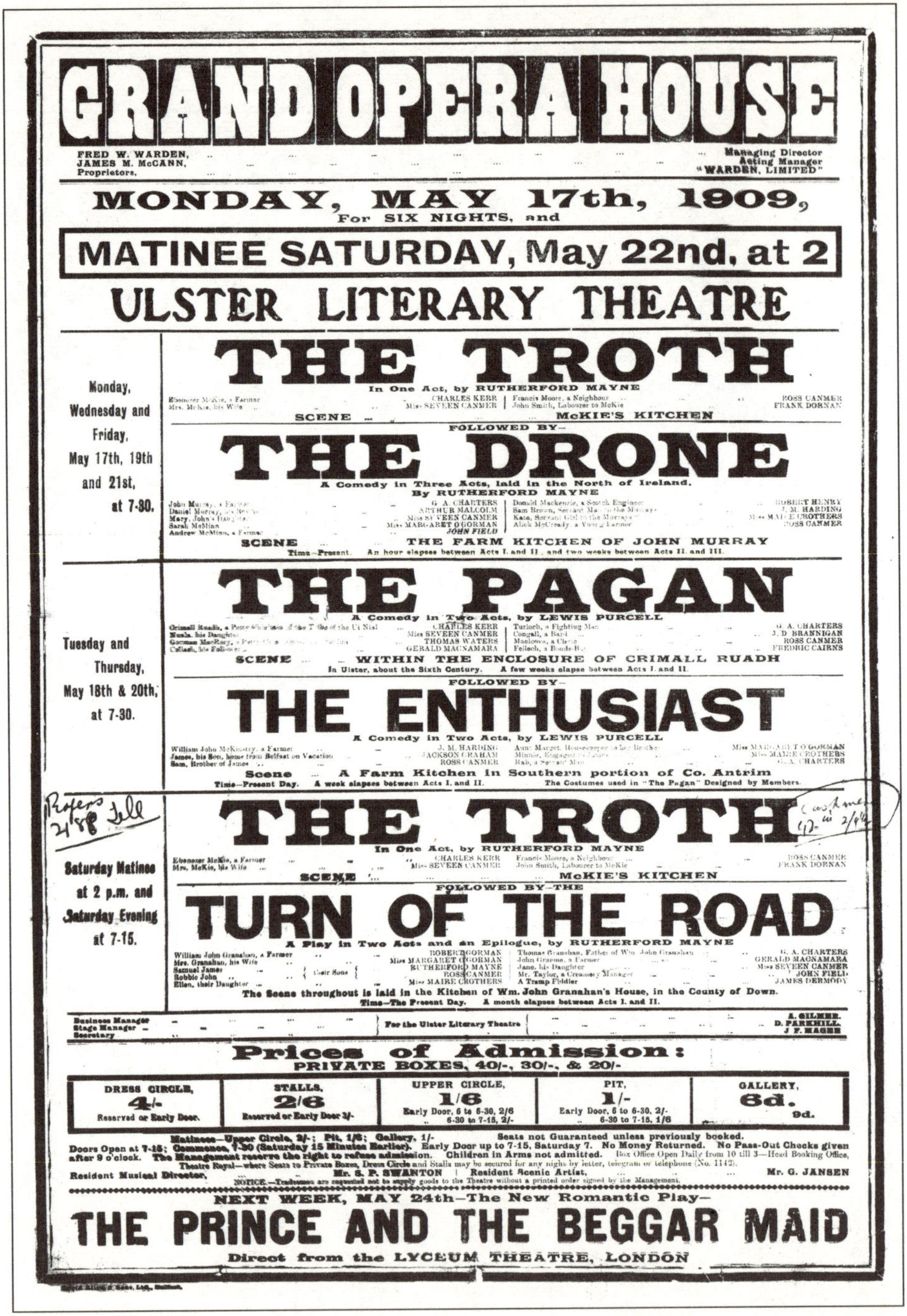

GRAND OPERA HOUSE

FRED W. WARDEN, JAMES M. McCANN, Proprietors. ... Managing Director, Acting Manager "WARDEN, LIMITED"

MONDAY, MAY 17th, 1909,

For SIX NIGHTS, and

MATINEE SATURDAY, May 22nd, at 2

ULSTER LITERARY THEATRE

Monday, Wednesday and Friday, May 17th, 19th and 21st, at 7-30.

THE TROTH

In One Act, by RUTHERFORD MAYNE

Ebenezer McKie, a Farmer	CHARLES KERR
Mrs. McKie, his Wife	Miss SEVEEN CANMER
Francis Moore, a Neighbour	ROSS CANMER
John Smith, Labourer to McKie	FRANK DORNAN

SCENE ... McKIE'S KITCHEN

FOLLOWED BY–

THE DRONE

A Comedy in Three Acts, laid in the North of Ireland, By RUTHERFORD MAYNE

John Murray, a Farmer	G. A. CHARTERS
Daniel Murray, his Brother	ARTHUR MALCOLM
Mary, John's Daughter	Miss SEVEEN CANMER
Sarah McMinn	Miss MARGARET O'GORMAN
Andrew McMinn, a Farmer	JOHN FIELD
Donald Mackenzie, a Scotch Engineer	ROBERT HENRY
Sam Brown, Servant Man to the Murrays	J. M. HARDING
Kate, Servant Girl to the Murrays	Miss MAIRE CROTHERS
Alick McCready, a Young Farmer	ROSS CANMER

SCENE ... THE FARM KITCHEN OF JOHN MURRAY

Time–Present. An hour elapses between Acts I. and II., and two weeks between Acts II. and III.

Tuesday and Thursday, May 18th & 20th, at 7-30.

THE PAGAN

A Comedy in Two Acts, by LEWIS PURCELL

Crimall Ruadh, a [illegible] of the Ui Nial	CHARLES KERR
Nuala, his Daughter	Miss SEVEEN CANMER
Gorman MacRory, a [illegible]	THOMAS WATERS
Colladh, his Follower	GERALD MACNAMARA
Turloch, a Fighting Man	G. A. CHARTERS
Congall, a Bard	J. D. BRANNIGAN
Maeleova, a Cleric	ROSS CANMER
Feilech, a Bonds-B[illegible]	FREDRIC CAIRNS

SCENE ... WITHIN THE ENCLOSURE OF CRIMALL RUADH

In Ulster, about the Sixth Century. A few weeks elapse between Acts I. and II.

FOLLOWED BY–

THE ENTHUSIAST

A Comedy in Two Acts, by LEWIS PURCELL

William John McKinstry, a Farmer	J. M. HARDING
James, his Son, home from Belfast on Vacation	JACKSON GRAHAM
Sam, Brother of James	ROSS CANMER
Aunt Marget, Housekeeper to her Brother	Miss MARGARET O'GORMAN
Minnie, Engaged to James	Miss MAIRE CROTHERS
Rab, a Servant Man	G. A. CHARTERS

Scene ... A Farm Kitchen in Southern portion of Co. Antrim

Time–Present Day. A week elapses between Acts I. and II. The Costumes used in "The Pagan" Designed by Members.

Rofers 21/88 [illegible]

Saturday Matinee at 2 p.m. and Saturday Evening at 7-15.

THE TROTH

In One Act, by RUTHERFORD MAYNE

Costumes 17- in 2/4[illegible]

Ebenezer McKie, a Farmer	CHARLES KERR
Mrs. McKie, his Wife	Miss SEVEEN CANMER
Francis Moore, a Neighbour	ROSS CANMER
John Smith, Labourer to McKie	FRANK DORNAN

SCENE ... McKIE'S KITCHEN

FOLLOWED BY–THE

TURN OF THE ROAD

A Play in Two Acts and an Epilogue, by RUTHERFORD MAYNE

William John Granahan, a Farmer	ROBERT GORMAN
Mrs. Granahan, his Wife	Miss MARGARET O'GORMAN
Samuel James } their Sons	RUTHERFORD MAYNE
Robbie John } their Sons	ROSS CANMER
Ellen, their Daughter	Miss MAIRE CROTHERS
Thomas Granahan, Father of Wm. John Granahan	G. A. CHARTERS
John Graeme, a Farmer	GERALD MACNAMARA
Jane, his Daughter	Miss SEVEEN CANMER
Mr. Taylor, a Creamery Manager	JOHN FIELD
A Tramp Fiddler	JAMES DERMODY

The Scene throughout is laid in the Kitchen of Wm. John Granahan's House, in the County of Down.

Time–The Present Day. A month elapses between Acts I. and II.

Business Manager	For the Ulster Literary Theatre	A. GILMER.
Stage Manager		D. PARKHILL.
Secretary		J. F. MAGEE

Prices of Admission:

PRIVATE BOXES, 40/-, 30/-, & 20/-

DRESS CIRCLE,	STALLS,	UPPER CIRCLE,	PIT,	GALLERY,
4/- Reserved or Early Door.	2/6 Reserved or Early Door 3/-	1/6 Early Door, 6 to 6-30, 2/6; 6-30 to 7-15, 2/-	1/- Early Door, 6 to 6-30, 2/-; 6-30 to 7-15, 1/6	6d. 9d.

Matinees–Upper Circle, 2/-; Pit, 1/6; Gallery, 1/- Seats not Guaranteed unless previously booked.
Doors Open at 7-15; Commence, 7-30 (Saturday 15 Minutes Earlier). Early Door up to 7-15, Saturday 7. No Money Returned. No Pass-Out Checks given after 9 o'clock. The Management reserve the right to refuse admission. Children in Arms not admitted. Box Office Open Daily from 10 till 3–Head Booking Office, Theatre Royal–where Seats to Private Boxes, Dress Circle and Stalls may be secured for any night by letter, telegram or telephone (No. 1142).
Resident Musical Director, ... Mr. S. P. SWANTON | Resident Scenic Artist, ... Mr. G. JANSEN
NOTICE.–Tradesmen are requested not to supply goods to the Theatre without a printed order signed by the Management.

NEXT WEEK, MAY 24th–The New Romantic Play–

THE PRINCE AND THE BEGGAR MAID

Direct from the LYCEUM THEATRE, LONDON

First Productions of the Ulster Literary Theatre

researched by **Ophelia Byrne**

Play, Writer, Date, Location

The Reformers, Lewis Purcell, 7th December 1904, Ulster Minor Hall, Belfast

Brian of Banba, Bulmer Hobson, 7th December 1904, Ulster Minor Hall, Belfast

Little Cowherd of Slainge, Seosamh MacCathmhaoil, 4th May 1905, Clarence Place Hall, Belfast

The Enthusiast, Lewis Purcell, 4th May 1905, Clarence Place Hall, Belfast

The Turn of the Road, Rutherford Mayne, 4th December 1906, Examination Hall, Queen's College Belfast

The Pagan, Lewis Purcell, 4th December 1906, Examination Hall, Queen's College Belfast

Suzanne and the Sovereigns, Gerald MacNamara and Lewis Purcell, 26th December 1907, Exhibition Hall, Belfast

The Drone, Rutherford Mayne, 24th April 1908, Abbey Theatre, Dublin

Leaders of the People, Robert Harding, 24th April 1908, Abbey Theatre, Dublin

The Mist That Does Be On the Bog, Gerald MacNamara, 26th November 1909, Abbey Theatre, Dublin

Captain of the Hosts, Rutherford Mayne, 8th March 1910, Grand Opera House

Charity, Miss M.F. Scott, 4th December 1911, Grand Opera House, Belfast

Red Turf, Rutherford Mayne, 5th December 1911, Grand Opera House, Belfast

The Jerry Builders, William Paul, 5th December 1911, Grand Opera House, Belfast

Thompson in Tir-na-nOg, Gerald MacNamara, 9th December 1912, Grand Opera House, Belfast

Family Rights, Miss M.F. Scott, 9th December 1912, Grand Opera House, Belfast

Sweeping the Country, William Paul, 10th December 1912, Grand Opera House, Belfast

Love and Land, Lynn Doyle, 24th November 1913, Grand Opera House

If, Rutherford Mayne, 25th November 1913, Grand Opera House

Evening, Rutherford Mayne, 2nd March 1914, Grand Opera House

Snowdrop Jane, Shaun F. Bullock, 2nd February 1915, Grand Opera House, Belfast

The Spoiled Buddha, Helen Waddell, 1st February 1915, Grand Opera House, Belfast

The Old Lady, Bernard Duffy, 11th December 1916, Grand Opera House, Belfast

The Tumelty Case, William Paul, 13th December 1916, Grand Opera House, Belfast

The Throwbacks, Gerald MacNamara, 3rd December 1917, Grand Opera House, Belfast

The Dark Hour, Robert Christie, 3rd December 1917,
Grand Opera House, Belfast

Industry, Rutherford Mayne, 6th December 1917,
Grand Opera House, Belfast

The Skipper's Submarine, Charles K. Ayre, 6th December 1917,
Grand Opera House, Belfast

The Summons, Lynn Doyle, 25-Mar-1918, Grand Opera House, Belfast

Sincerity, Gerald MacNamara, 31st May 1918, Gaiety Theatre, Dublin

Away from the Moss, George S. Morshiel, 25th November 1918,
Grand Opera House, Belfast

The Lilac Ribbon, Lynn Doyle, 5the June 1919, Grand Opera House, Belfast

Felix Reid and Bob, George S. Morshiel, 12th November 1919,
Grand Opera House, Belfast

The Lone Man, Charles K. Ayre, 14th November 1919,
Grand Opera House, Belfast

The Jew's Fiddle, H. Richard Hayward and Abram Rish,
18th December 1920, Gaiety Theatre, Dublin

Loaves and Fishes, Charles K. Ayre, 2nd November 1921,
Grand Opera House, Belfast

Turncoats, Lynn Doyle, 4th September 1922, Liverpool Play House

Fee-Faw-Fum, Gerald MacNamara, 2nd April 1923, Opera House, Derry

Phantoms, Rutherford Mayne, 28th November 1923, Gaiety Theatre, Dublin

The Land of the Stranger, Dorothea Donn-Byrne, 8th December 1924,
Gaiety Theatre, Dublin

The Ship, St. John Ervine, 10th December 1924, Gaiety Theatre, Dublin

Huge Love, Richard Hayward, 10th December 1924, Gaiety Theatre, Dublin

Missing Links, Charles K. Ayre, 15th December 1925,
Gaiety Theatre, Dublin

No Surrender, Gerald MacNamara, 23rd January 1928,
Grand Opera House, Belfast

Who Fears to Speak, Gerald MacNamara, 24th January 1929,
Grand Opera House, Belfast

The Delph Dog, Larry Morrow, 21st September 1931,
Grand Opera House, Belfast

Cobbers Go Halves, Lewis Purcell, 24th September 1931,
Grand Opera House, Belfast

A Majority of One, William Liddell, 11th June 1934,
Grand Opera House, Belfast

The Ball Turns Once, Jack Loudan, 14th June 1934,
Grand Opera House, Belfast

Thompson on Terra Firma, Gerald MacNamara, nd/nd/1934,
Grand Opera House, Belfast

Permission to reproduce this list was kindly given by
www.irishplayography.com
A comprehensive database of new Irish plays produced professionally
in Ireland, North and South.

Further Reading

The Stage in Ulster from the Eighteenth Century (1997) by Ophelia Byrne.
The Ulster Theatre in Ireland (1931) by Margaret McHenry.
The Theatre in Ulster (1972) by Sam Hanna Bell.
Sam Thompson and Modern Drama in Ulster (1986) by Hagal Mengel.
The Girls in the Big Picture (2003) by Imelda Foley.